D1393461

Creative Ideas for Evening Prayer

Jan Brind
and
Tessa Wilkinson

CANTERBURY
PRESS
Norwich

Dedicated with love and thanks to our husbands, Robin and Guy, for their inspiration and encouragement, and to all who have stopped awhile and broken bread with us on the way.

With thanks also to family and friends for their support and advice, in particular Andrew and Wendy Bryant, St Mary the Virgin, Worplesden; Paul Jenkins, St Columba's House, Woking; and Carol Winterburn, Emmanuel Church, South Croydon (www.biggerpicture.org.uk).

© Jan Brind and Tessa Wilkinson 2005

First published in 2005 by the Canterbury Press Norwich
(a publishing imprint of Hymns Ancient & Modern Limited,
a registered charity)
13–17 Long Lane, London EC1A 9PN

www.scm-canterburypress.co.uk

Second impression, with CD
Third impression

British Library Cataloguing in Publication data

A catalogue record for this book is available
from the British Library.

ISBN 978 1 85311 924 8

Typeset by Regent Typesetting, London
Printed and bound by
MPG Books Ltd, Bodmin, Cornwall

CONTENTS

THE SERVICES

INTRODUCTION

It seems a great sadness that so often today the celebration of Evening Prayer has become a rare thing, or at best occasional, in the life of a parish. It tends either to attract a handful of people and seems an effort to keep going or, because there are so few people coming, it has vanished all together. In this book we hope to re-kindle enthusiasm for a service that happens during an evening. It may well be a Sunday evening, but it could just as easily be any day of the week. These days there are many things competing for people's time on a Sunday morning. It may be the only morning that it is possible to have a lie-in, or the children want to play football, or many families now do their big weekly shop together at the super-market. Rather than haranguing them for not coming to church on Sunday morn-ing, why not offer them an alternative time during an evening?

The themed worship we suggest does not follow the pattern of the traditional 'Evensong' service as given in *The Book of Common Prayer*, or the more recent services in *Common Worship*, but something more creative. We are not being constrained by a set approved liturgy, but rather we are allowing creativity to fly free so that we can really explore the many and wonderful ways to worship God.

Some of the services are quiet and meditative, while others are full of action and activity. For some we suggest staying in one place and for others we suggest moving around the church or building. Some may be aimed at those younger at heart, though all are aimed at anyone who loves to explore new approaches to worshipping their Lord. All of the services are themed to be used on a particular occasion. This occasion could be during a season that falls in the liturgical calen-dar, such as Pentecost, or to focus on a particular theme, for example Peace, or to acknowledge a situation in the world such as the campaign for Trade Justice. Some are designed for those moments when a particular event has happened and the church needs to respond immediately – a national disaster, for example. The Evening Prayer designed to respond to a natural disaster was written, and used, in the wake of the Asian tsunami. All are Bible-based and have God at their centre. The use of contemporary technology is not shied away from, but for those who are not confident in the use of computers or PowerPoint presentations there are plenty of creative ideas.

Hospitality is at the root of the Christian faith and we suggest that most, if not all, of these evenings should end with coffee and refreshments so that people can meet each other. Occasionally it may be appropriate to gather together at the start of the evening with coffee so that the service may end in quietness. On these occasions try not to hurry people away but allow them to leave in their own time.

These are services that can be led by lay people as well as clergy. Many people in parish congregations have the potential to lead worship. This is often an unexplored and undiscovered area of lay ministry. In some places there is specific training for worship leaders. However, even with no special training, we hope that the services in this book will encourage people to offer their gifts in this way. So often we expect our minister to always be at the front leading the worship. How good it is when he or she can come and enjoy a service without the responsibility for planning and leading it – just once in a while!

If there are new songs to sing, try teaching them before the service begins. Believe in people's ability to pick up new things. If you are singing unaccompanied don't pitch tunes too high to sing comfortably. Don't hide behind a microphone, unless you are using a loop system. Your singing does not have to be perfect. Make yourself vulnerable. Try signing the song in the air by moving one hand up and down with the notes as you sing. Practise in front of a mirror. If the song is completely unknown just teach the chorus in the first instance – line by line if necessary. Or sing new words to a familiar tune. Most songs have a metre written at the top – for example 87 87. If you look in the back of many hymnbooks you will find a metrical index of tunes. Find the list of tunes that go with the required metre and choose a tune that is well-known for the new song. Using responsorial material is a good way to engage the congregation – not just in psalms but in some newer songs as well. In many of our services we have given suggestions for two songs where songs are called for – often one that is easily accessible and an alternative that may be more challenging to find. But please do choose your own songs – these are only suggestions and are our own choices. The songs chosen may be in more than one book.

Copyright permission is important. Please make sure that you have up to date licences to cover the songs you use. The Christian Copyright Licence does not cover everything. A licence to cover many of the songs from Catholic composers can be obtained from Calamus, Decani Music, Oak House, 70 High Street, Brandon, Suffolk IP27 0AU. Calamus also administer a licence that covers songs from the Taizé Community.

The music we have chosen to play during some of the liturgies is music we particularly think fits the theme, and which we have to hand. You may have other recordings that would work just as well.

There is a separate chapter on the use of worship space. You may have a church you can use, or you may well choose to use a hall or other building – or even be outdoors!

We have also written separately about ways to make these services fully accessible to those with impairment or disability and the importance of using language that includes rather than excludes.

We have made a list of things it would be useful to collect and store in a Resource Cupboard. And, where there are things to make, illustration templates and instructions are included at the back of the book for ease of photocopying.

The Bibles we have used are the New International Version, New Revised Standard Version and Good News Bible. We have also sometimes used The Message Remix by Eugene H. Peterson published in 2003 by NavPress Publishing Group.

Please note that where 'all' are invited to participate in the liturgy this is indicated by bold type.

Finally, please use these service outlines as just that – outlines. Feel free to adapt and change them to fit your own creative ideas. We hope that this book might give you the courage to invite God to move among you to 'do a new thing'.

WORSHIP SPACE

Where to meet

The area where you choose to hold your Evening Prayer will vary enormously. It might be a large, lofty Victorian church or someone's sitting room. It might be a modern church or an ancient church, or it might be in a garden or a tent. It really does not matter where the space is, or even what it looks like, because it can always be prepared to suit the occasion. What is much more important is that it is a defined area where people can gather together undisturbed to worship their Lord and God.

Lighting

One of the things that has the greatest impact on the feel and atmosphere of a service is the lighting. Bright lights will encourage people to be alert and loud, whereas low dim lights can create an atmosphere of stillness and calm. If the space only has overhead lights which are unadjustable, either on full or off, it is always worth considering bringing in some lamp stands with low voltage bulbs. These, with careful placing, can completely change the atmosphere. In most of the services we suggest candles of differing sizes being used as these give off a very gentle soft light, again adding to the atmosphere. But make sure that the lights are not too dim, so making it difficult for people to read the words on the service sheet. Getting the balance right between enough light to read by, but not too much to make it too bright, is important. Always allow enough time before the service starts to see that the lighting is providing the right atmosphere. Remember that in the summer months it may be light when the service starts, but become dark during the service.

The lights can often be used to define the prayer space. Much of the church can be left in darkness as if it were not there, and then when people arrive, they will be drawn towards the lighted area, which will encourage them to sit together.

Temperature

If people are cold they will not be able to concentrate on the worship so, if possible, always try to make the worship space warm. If the church is enormous and difficult to heat try to use a small part and heat that with electric heaters or gas bottle fires. Sometimes side chapels or the sanctuary are easier to heat and a good space for a smaller group of people to gather. But do not dismiss using the hall or a meeting room. With some imagination these can easily be transformed into a space for worship. Being warm can be more important than being in the church building. Obviously the same applies to being too warm. This may be one of those occasions when worship can take place outside in the cool of the evening. Or the church doors can be thrown open to allow the cool air to come in. This may also encourage people to walk through the door as they will be able to see what is going on inside.

Arranging the space

In most of the services in this book we have suggested that people should gather round a focal point, often in the round, or in a semi-circle, sitting on chairs, or the floor. Allow enough space so that people are not on top of one another, but always encourage people to sit together. These are not occasions for people to sit in 'their' pews scattered in all four corners of the church building. If the building only has pews, then only offer people seats in the front few rows and rope off the pews further back so that people have to sit up at the front together.

It may be worth considering defining the space with rugs or cushions on the floor. We are not often invited to sit on the floor in church, but being down low on a cushion can offer freedom from the constraints of being seated on a hard uncomfortable chair or pew. Prayer stools can also be used, so bringing people much closer to the focal point. Rugs and cushions also have the advantage of taking people off the floor which may be very cold to sit on.

The focal point

This is the area where the focus of the evening will take place. It might contain a large cross, pictures, a map, or the names of places being prayed for. Whatever the theme of the evening, it will be illustrated at this point in the church. The people attending will probably sit facing this area. Whatever is being used should be displayed beautifully. This is being done to the glory of God, so it should reflect our best efforts. Flowers or greenery might be used to enhance the display. Candles are often placed among the items. Having candles at different heights is also good, some in candlesticks and some small nightlights lower down.

The display needs to be thought through carefully. The purpose of it is to focus people's minds on the theme for the service, and to help lead them into prayer. It should not act as a distraction, so it should not be fussy. It might simply be one picture, or one word. Suggestions have been made at the beginning of each service.

Movement

Having decided where to focus the worship it is also important to think about how the space will work, particularly if there is an 'action' that takes place in the service, when the congregation is invited to get up and do something. Check to see that the candles are not placed in such a way as to be a fire hazard. Make sure that there is enough space between the chairs so that people can get to the focal point without having to climb over each other. If people are in pews the 'action' may, instead, have to be taken to the people. So, rather than inviting everyone to go to the front, a container or basket with, for example, cards or bread, may be passed along the rows of pews, so that everyone feels involved. Always be mindful of those who may find it difficult to move around or bend down.

Music

If there is going to be recorded music used during the service, make sure that the CD player works and check the sound levels. Remember that when a space is filled with people they will act as a barrier to sound, so the music may need to be played louder when the congregation is in place. Make sure that the CD to be used is marked clearly. A 'post-it' note with the track number to be used marked clearly on it will help, especially if several CDs are to be used during the service.

Think carefully where the person leading the singing should sit. In a quiet service it may be that he or she can sit among the people, just as part of the group. Tuning forks or a small keyboard may be used to give the notes at the beginning of a song. Keep it all very simple. It may well be unnecessary to have a piano or organ. Think about using other instruments – a flute works beautifully. If the group has no one able to lead the singing then use pre-recorded music. This can either be listened to or people can sing along with the CD.

ALL ARE WELCOME

All our worship spaces, whether in ancient or modern churches or buildings, should be places of warm welcome and hospitality. We do not expect visitors to our homes to be cold or uncomfortable – we go out of our way to make our families and friends feel wanted and at ease. Many of our worship places have limitations when it comes to providing comfortable and prayerful space. Some of our ancient buildings, with small congregations, find it difficult to raise money for new heating, modern equipment and building work. And yet, churches should be places where all God's family feel at home.

This book is about Evening Prayer. Services in the evening have obvious advantages as we mention in the Introduction. However, they also pose some problems for some people. In the winter, when evenings are dark, a lot of people are anxious about coming out especially if driving is involved. Can lifts be offered to people who might not otherwise be able to come? Public transport on Sunday evenings is often limited.

When we welcome people to share in our worship it is important that we are mindful of the needs of those who may find it difficult to join in. Sometimes, quite subconsciously, with the words we use or the actions we plan, we fail to consider the needs of those with physical, mental, sensory, or learning impairment. Impairment should not necessarily mean 'disability' within our places of worship. Churches should be 'open to all' in terms of access and participation.

So what can we do to make our worship spaces accessible and welcoming to all who want to use them?

Dioceses across the country have responded in differing ways to the recent Disability Discrimination Act. There is almost certainly someone in your diocese, a disability advisor, or local authority access officer, who has special responsibility for advising parishes on accessibility for all. Wheelchair users need to be able to get into the church building, or at least into the part of the building where the worship is to be held, before they can participate. Most churches have now made provision for wheelchair access, but it is worth checking. If there are cloakrooms, are they well-marked, lit and accessible?

Are there reserved car parking spaces near to the building for those who need them? Are the car park and the path well-lit in winter months?

White lines drawn on steps make them visible to people who have failing eyesight. Again, this is particularly important in the winter months.

Large print copies of the liturgy in 18 pt might be helpful to some. Certain fonts are easier to read than others. Use 12 pt in a clear font such as Arial, Helvetica, Times New Roman or Universal. Black print on plain white or pale yellow paper is helpful to everyone. Avoid strong colours such as red, dark green or dark blue. Use bold lower case for print that everyone is to read rather than capital letters. Is there enough light in the building for people to read without straining?

Many churches now have induction loop systems installed. Is this well advertised for those who wear hearing aids? Is the area you plan to use accessible to the hearing loop? Might there be someone in the congregation who can use British Sign Language? It is helpful to all of us if a reader's face is well-lit and not in shadow. We all find it easier to hear if we can watch a reader's lips.

Language matters. Words can be carefully chosen to be inclusive – not only in our daily conversations but within our liturgy. Carelessly chosen words can sometimes bring pain and hurt to people hearing or reading them and cannot be undone. The language we use reflects our attitudes. Do we use language that is understandable and includes, or do we use jargon that excludes? Many words that are used in our liturgy are a complete mystery to those visiting our churches, maybe for the first time and, although God is a mysterious God, do we really want the mystery of the liturgy to inhibit our worship? We want to create simple liturgy that inspires – and this does not mean it has to be simplistic.

Music is very important in our liturgy. It connects directly with, and feeds, the spirit. Choose music that reflects and relates to the atmosphere of the liturgy.

Corporate silence can be powerful. Warn people that there will be silence when this is appropriate. Silence of an 'unknown' length can be difficult for some people. And feel the silence – if there is general restlessness draw it to a close after a short time.

When we want someone to take an active part in a service, either by reading something or moving from their seat, it is a good idea to ask them quietly beforehand. Or, better still, ask generally 'Is there someone here who would like to read?' Never put someone on the spot. Asking a group to read verses from the Bible in turn can cause great discomfort and anxiety for someone who finds reading difficult.

Are there candles to light? If so, make sure that some of them are on a low table which is high enough for everyone to reach. Some of us find it difficult bending down to the floor. Make sure no one is excluded from lighting a candle if they wish to. Help each other. Be aware of safety.

Are there stones to pick up, or chains to break, or some other action, as part of the liturgy? Again, make sure these things are accessible to all, and not all at floor level. Pass a basket around if this is easier.

Very often in our eucharistic services we see those who are unable to access the altar rail receive communion after everyone else. It might be good sometimes if people with impairment or disability were chosen to be first, rather than last. Perhaps we can bear this in mind in our evening liturgies when there are things to give or receive.

Are there words to write? Always give people the option of drawing.

If there are things to pin on a board, use an easel or notice board that is steady and easy to reach.

Burning incense can have a beneficial effect on the senses, and help to create an atmosphere of healing and prayer, but it can also sometimes aggravate asthma in some people. So be aware of this. As an alternative, incense sticks or aroma-therapy oil in a burner, or an aromatherapy spray, can be used. Lavender and rosemary work well. Allowing incense to burn before the Evening Prayer begins so that people come into a scented atmosphere is another way of using our sense of smell.

Touch – not everyone likes to be touched, or held. Be aware of this when suggesting, for example, that everyone holds hands as part of a liturgy.

Many people whom society generally might consider to have 'impairment' or 'disability' consider themselves to have no such thing! It is very often those who think they are 'whole' who give people who are different these titles. By being aware of the needs of the people we would like to draw together for an evening gathering, the space we create, the atmosphere within that space, the words we use, the actions we propose, the music and the silence we plan, and the hospitality we offer, we will go some way towards being the inclusive church that Jesus might recognize.

A SELECTION OF RESOURCE BOOKS

These might be helpful when planning evening liturgy

A Wee Worship Book, Wild Goose Worship Group, Wild Goose Publications, 1999.

Alternative Worship, Compiled by Jonny Baker and Doug Gay with Jenny Brown, SPCK, 2003.

Approaches to Prayer: A resource book for groups and individuals, edited by Henry Morgan, SPCK, 1991.

Bread of Tomorrow: Praying with the world's poor, edited by Janet Morley, SPCK and Christian Aid, 1992.

Celtic Daily Prayer, The Northumbria Community, HarperCollins*Religious*, 2000.

Celtic Worship: Through the year, Ray Simpson, Hodder and Stoughton, 1997.

Cloth for the Cradle: Worship resources and readings for Advent, Christmas and Epiphany, Wild Goose Worship Group, Wild Goose Resource Group, Wild Goose Publications, 1997.

Crafts for Creative Worship: A resource and activity book for parishes, Jan Brind and Tessa Wilkinson, Canterbury Press, 2004.

Freedom in Worship: Building a creative blend of the old and the new, Tim Lomax, Kevin Mayhew, 2001.

Freedom Within a Framework: Breathing new life into liturgy, Tim Lomax, Kevin Mayhew, 2001.

Great Celtic Christians: Alternative worship from the Community of Aidan and Hilda, Ray Simpson, Kevin Mayhew, 2004.

Harvest for the World: A worship anthology on sharing in the work of creation, compiled by Geoffrey Duncan for Christian Aid, Canterbury Press, 2002.

Healing the Land: Natural seasons, sacraments and special services, Ray Simpson, Kevin Mayhew, 2004.

In this Hour – Liturgies for Pausing, Dorothy McRae-McMahon, SPCK, 2001.

Iona Abbey Worship Book, compiled by the Iona Community, Wild Goose Publications, 2001.

Let Justice Roll Down: A Christian Aid/CAFOD anthology for Lent, Holy Week and Easter, compiled by Geoffrey Duncan, Canterbury Press, 2003.

Liturgies for the Journey of Life, Dorothy McRae-McMahon, SPCK, 2000.

Making Liturgy: Creating rituals for worship and life, edited by Dorothea McEwan, Pat Pinsent, Ianthe Pratt and Veronica Seddon, Canterbury Press, 2001.

Multi-Sensory Prayer, Sue Wallace, Scripture Union, 2000.

New Patterns for Worship, The Archbishops' Council, Church House Publishing, 2002.

One Lord, One Faith: Ecumenical services for the Christian year, Stuart Thomas, Kevin Mayhew, 2000.

Out of the Ordinary: prayers, poems and reflections for every season, Joyce Rupp, Ave Maria Press, 2000.

Prayer for Each Day, Taizé Community, Cassell, 1997.

Prayer Rhythms: Fourfold patterns for each day, Ray Simpson, Kevin Mayhew, 2003.

Prayers Encircling the World: An international anthology of 300 contemporary prayers, compiled by SPCK, SPCK, 1998.

Prayers for Life's Particular Moments, Dorothy McRae-McMahon, SPCK, 2001.

Present on Earth: Worship resources on the life of Jesus, Wild Goose Worship Group, Wild Goose Resource Group, Wild Goose Publications, 2002.

Seeing Christ in Others, edited by Geoffrey Duncan, Canterbury Press, 2002.

Shine on Star of Bethlehem: A worship resource for Advent, Christmas and Epiphany, compiled by Geoffrey Duncan for Christian Aid, Canterbury Press, 2001.

Stages on the Way: Worship resources for Lent, Holy Week and Easter, Wild Goose Worship Group, Wild Goose Resource Group, Wild Goose Publications, 1998.

Take, Bless, Break, Share: Agapes, table blessings and liturgies, Simon Bryden-Brook, Canterbury Press, 1998.

The Rhythm of Life: Celtic daily prayer, David Adam, SPCK, 1996.

Watching for the Kingfisher, Ann Lewin, Inspire, 2004.

Words by the Way, Ann Lewin, Inspire, 2005.

A SELECTION OF
HYMNBOOKS AND
SONG BOOKS

CDs or cassettes are available for titles marked with an asterisk

Be Still and Know, compiled by Margaret Rizza, Kevin Mayhew, 2000.

Beneath a Travelling Star, Timothy Dudley-Smith, Canterbury Press, 2001.

Cantate: A book of short chants, hymns, responses and litanies, edited by Stephen Dean, Decani Music, 2005.

Celebration Hymnal for Everyone, edited by Patrick Geary, McCrimmons Publishing, 1994.

*Christ Be Our Light, Bernadette Farrell, OCP Publications, 1994 (available from Decani Music).

Church Hymnary – Fourth Edition, editorial panel convened by the Church of Scotland and led by John L. Bell and Charles Robertson, Canterbury Press, 2005.

*Come All You People: Shorter songs for worship, John L. Bell, Wild Goose Publications, 1994.

*Common Ground: A song book for all the churches, John L. Bell and editorial committee, Saint Andrew Press, 1998.

Common Praise, compiled by Hymns Ancient and Modern Ltd, Canterbury Press, 2000.

Complete Anglican Hymns Old and New, compiled by Geoffrey Moore, Susan Sayers, Michael Forster and Kevin Mayhew, Kevin Mayhew, 2000.

**Drawn to Wonder: Hymns and songs from churches worldwide*, compiled by Francis Brienen and Maggie Hamilton, Council for World Mission, 1995.

Enemy of Apathy, John L. Bell and Graham Maule, Wild Goose Publications, 1988 (revised 1990).

*Fire of Love, Margaret Rizza, Kevin Mayhew, 1998.

*Fountain of Life, Margaret Rizza, Kevin Mayhew, 1997.

Gather – Second Edition, edited by Robert J. Batastini, GIA Publications, 1994.

Gift of God, Marty Haugen, GIA Publications, 2001.

Glory and Praise – Second Edition, Oregon Catholic Press, 2000.

*Go Before Us, Bernadette Farrell, OCP Publications, 2003 (available from Decani Music).

**God Beyond All Names*, Bernadette Farrell, OCP Publications, 1991 (available from Decani Music).

**Heaven Shall Not Wait*, John L. Bell and Graham Maule, Wild Goose Publications, 1987 (reprinted 1994).

Hymns and Psalms, British Methodist Conference, Methodist Publishing House, 1987.

Hymns Old and New: New Anglican Edition, compiled by Geoffrey Moore, Susan Sayers, Michael Foster and Kevin Mayhew, Kevin Mayhew, 1996.

Hymns Old and New: One church, one faith, one Lord, compiled by Colin Mawby, Kevin Mayhew, Susan Sayers, Ray Simpson and Stuart Thomas, Kevin Mayhew, 2004.

I Will Not Sing Alone, John L. Bell, Wild Goose Publications, 2004.

Innkeepers and Light Sleepers: Songs for Christmas, John L. Bell, Wild Goose Publications, 1992.

Iona Abbey Music Book: Songs from the Iona Abbey Worship Book, compiled by the Iona Community, Wild Goose Publications, 2003.

Light in Our Darkness, Margaret Rizza, Kevin Mayhew, 2002.

Laudate, edited by Stephen Dean, Decani Music, 2000.

Liturgical Hymns Old and New, compiled by Robert Kelly, Sister Sheila McGovern SSL, Kevin Mayhew, Father Andrew Moore and Sister Louisa Poole SSL, Kevin Mayhew, 1999.

Love + Anger: Songs of lively faith and social justice, John L. Bell and Graham Maule, Wild Goose Publications, 1997.

Love from Below, John L. Bell and Graham Maule, Wild Goose Publications, 1989.

Many and Great: World church songs (vol. 1), John L. Bell and Graham Maule, Wild Goose Publications, 1990 .

Methodist Hymns Old and New, compiled by Revd Peter Bolt, Revd Amos Cresswell, Mrs Tracy Harding and Revd Ray Short, Kevin Mayhew, 2001.

Mission Praise, compiled by Roland Fudge, Peter Horrobin and Greg Leavers, Marshall Pickering, 1983.

New Hymns and Worship Songs, Kevin Mayhew, 2001.

New Start Hymns and Songs, compiled by Kevin Mayhew, Kevin Mayhew, 1999.

One Is the Body: Songs of unity and diversity, John L. Bell, Wild Goose Publications, 2002.

Psalms of Patience, Protest and Praise: 23 psalm settings, John L. Bell, Wild Goose Publications, 1993.

Rejoice and Sing, Oxford University Press, 1991.

Restless Is the Heart, Bernadette Farrell, OCP Publications, 2000 (available from Decani Music).

Resurrexit: Music for Lent, the Easter Triduum and Eastertide, edited by Stephen Dean, Decani Music, 2001.

River of Peace, Margaret Rizza, Kevin Mayhew, 1998.

Sent by the Lord: World church songs (vol. 2), John L. Bell and Graham Maule, Wild Goose Publications, 1991.

Share the Light, Bernadette Farrell, OCP Publications, 2000 (available from Decani Music).

Sing Glory: Hymns, psalms and songs for a new century, edited by Michael Baughen, Kevin Mayhew, 1999.

Songs and Prayers from Taizé, Ateliers et Presses de Taizé, Geoffrey Chapman Mowbray, 1991 (reprinted 1992).

Songs from Taizé, Ateliers et Presses de Taizé, published annually.

Songs of Fellowship, compiled by members of Kingsway Music editorial team, Kingsway Music, 1991.

Songs of God's People, the Panel on Worship, Church of Scotland, Oxford University Press, 1988 (reprinted 1995).

Taizé: Songs for prayer, instrumental edition, Ateliers et Presses de Taizé, HarperCollins, 2001.

Taizé: Songs for prayer, vocal edition, Ateliers et Presses de Taizé, HarperCollins, 1998.

Tales of Wonder, Marty Haugen, GIA Publications, 1989 (available from Decani Music).

The Courage to Say No: Songs for Lent and Easter, John L. Bell and Graham Maule, Wild Goose Publications, 1996.

The Last Journey: Reflections for the time of grieving, John L. Bell, Wild Goose Publications, 1996.

The Source: Definitive worship collection, compiled by Graham Kendrick, Kevin Mayhew, 1998.

There Is One Among Us: Shorter songs for worship, John L. Bell, Wild Goose Publications, 1998.

Turn My heart: Praying the sacred journey from brokenness to healing, Marty Haugen, GIA Publications, 2003 (available from Decani Music).

Veni Emmanuel: Music for Advent and Christmastide, edited by Stephen Dean, Decani Music, 2001.

Walk with Christ, Stephen Dean, OCP Publications, 1996 (available from Decani Music).

When Grief Is Raw: Songs for times of sorrow and bereavement, John L. Bell and Graham Maule, Wild Goose Publications, 1997.

World Praise, David Peacock and Geoff Weaver, Marshall Pickering, 1993.

Worship – Third Edition, edited by Robert J. Batastini, GIA Publications Inc., 1986.

21st Century Folk Hymnal, compiled by Kevin Mayhew, Kevin Mayhew, 1999.

THE RESOURCE CUPBOARD

Here is a list of useful resources to collect and keep – gradually add other things as you need them.

Access to a computer and printer
Access to the Internet
Access to a photocopier
Balloons
Baskets – different sizes
Bibles – several different translations
BluTack
Board – for mounting large sheets of paper
Books of prayers
Books of songs, hymns and psalms
Burner – for incense or fragrant oil
Candle holders – different sizes and heights
Candles – all sizes
Card – white and coloured
CD player and remote control
CDs – build up a collection

Charcoal briquettes
Clip Art CD
Coins
Collections of pictures – from cards, magazines and the press
Cushions
Double-sided tape
Drawing pins
Dried leaves
Drip shields
Easels
Extension lead
Fabric
Fishing net
Fragrant oils
Hammer and nails
Glue
Guillotine
Icons
Incense
Indoor water pump – from a garden centre
Jugs and water bowls
Labels – 'post-it notes'
Laminator

Laptop computer
Large cross
Lining paper
Low tables
Map of the world
Matches
Nightlights
Paschal candle
Pens and pencils
Plastic sheeting
PowerPoint projector and screen
Prayer stools
Rugs
Sand
Scissors
Shells
Stapler
Stones
String
Tapers
Torch
Towels
Whistles
White tiles
Wrapping paper

OUTLINE PATTERN FOR EVENING PRAYER

Here is an outline pattern that may help when planning a themed Evening Prayer. This is just a suggestion – be creative – but make sure that the gospel is at the heart of all you plan. Some of the included liturgies follow this pattern – some are slightly different – while some break this mould completely.

Before planning the Evening Prayer

- Choose a theme
- Find a relevant reading from the Bible that illustrates the theme
- Pick out a specific verse from the reading that encapsulates the theme
- Think how the space may be used creatively

Plan the Evening Prayer

- Welcome and explanation of the evening
- Opening prayer or Responses
- Song
- Psalm
- Reading – Bible or secular, or both
- Song
- Prayers
- Recorded music leading into silence
- Symbolic action
- Song
- Final prayer
- Sending out

RESOURCES USED AND ACKNOWLEDGEMENTS

Advent

Cloth for the Cradle, Wild Goose Publications, 1997.

After a Natural Disaster

The Epistle of Paul to the Romans, C. H. Dodd, Fontana Books, 1959.
'I said to the man who stood at the gate of the year', Minnie Louise Haskins.

All Saints

CD *God Beyond All Names*, Bernadette Farrell, OCP Publications.

All Souls

CD *Adagio for Strings*, Barber.
Bambi, Felix Salten, Ladybird Books, 2003.
'We can shed tears that they have gone' (Anon).

Baptism

Common Worship Service of Holy Baptism, Church House Publishing, 2000.
CD *Peer Gynt Suite No 1*, 'Morning', Grieg.

Blessing

CD *Fire of Love*, Margaret Rizza, Kevin Mayhew.
CD *Go Before Us*, Bernadette Farrell, OCP Publications.
Life of the Beloved, Henri Nouwen, Hodder and Stoughton, 1992.

Celebrating Community

CD *The Song and the Silence*, Marty Haugen, GIA Publications.

Christian Unity

CD *Laudate Omnes Gentes*, Taizé Community.
CD *Taizé Instrumental*, Taizé Community.

Cost of Discipleship

CD *God Beyond All Names*, Bernadette Farrell, OCP Publications.

Easter

CD *I Will Not Sing Alone*, The Wild Goose Collective and Macappella, Wild Goose Publications.

Epiphany

CD *Icons*, Margaret Rizza, Kevin Mayhew.
Imagining God, Trevor Dennis, SPCK, 1997.
CD *One Bright Star*, Marty Haugen and Marc Anderson, GIA Publications.

Harvest of Creation

CD *Sacred Weave*, Keith Duke, Kevin Mayhew.
Song for Sarah, Paul D'Arcy, Lion Books, 1979.

Harvest of the Body of Christ

CD *River of Peace*, Margaret Rizza, Kevin Mayhew.
The Message, Eugene H. Peterson, NavPress Publishing Group, 2003.
CD *Laudate Omnes Gentes*, Taizé Community.
CD *Taizé Instrumental*, Taizé Community.

HIV/AIDS

CD *Turn My Heart*, Marty Haugen, GIA Publications.

Holy Week

CD *Sing to God*, Taizé Community.

Journeying

CD *Christ, Be Our Light*, Bernadette Farrell, OCP Publications.

Lent

CD *Gift of God*, Marty Haugen, GIA Publications.

Meeting Jesus Unexpectedly

CD *The Feast of Life*, Marty Haugen, GIA Publications.

Mental Health

CD *Fire of Love*, Margaret Rizza, Kevin Mayhew.

Midsummer

CD *Gloria – The Sacred Music of John Rutter*, Collegium Records.

National or International Tragedy

CD *Gift of God*, Marty Haugen, GIA Publications.

Peace

CD *Go Before Us*, Bernadette Farrell, OCP Publications.

Pentecost

CD *Go Before Us*, Bernadette Farrell, OCP Publications.

Prisoners

The Lion Prayer Collection, compiled by Mary Batchelor, Lion Publishing, 1992.
CD *River of Peace*, Margaret Rizza, Kevin Mayhew.
CD *The Sound of Kings*, Vaughan Williams, EMI.

Refugees and Asylum Seekers

CD *Godspell*, Arista Records.

The Lord's Prayer

CD *African Sanctus*, David Fanshawe, Philips.
CD *The Armed Man: A mass for peace*, Karl Jenkins, Virgin Records.
CD *Celtic Daily Prayer from the Northumbria Community*, CN Productions.
CD *Hopes and Dreams: A new musical for a new millennium*, Kingsway Music.
CD *Joy on Earth*, Taizé Community.
CD *The Lord's Prayer*, Ash Family and Friends, Hope Music, Guildford.
CD *Messiah*, Handel.

Trade Justice

CD *It Takes a Whole Village*, African Children's Choir.
Words of Wisdom, Jan Berry from *Harvest for the World*, Canterbury Press, 2002.

Water

Common Worship Service of Holy Baptism, Church House Publishing, 2000.

World Peace

CD *The Armed Man: A mass for peace*, Karl Jenkins, Virgin Records.

THE SERVICES

ADVENT

Here is a service outline for an evening in Advent using an idea from the Wild Goose Resource Group, Iona Community. The Iona Community is an ecumenical Christian community based in Glasgow. It is a dispersed community of ordained and lay people committed to seeking new ways of living the gospel in today's world. It focuses on issues of justice and peace, an ecumenical approach to inclusive worship, and the renewal of the church. The Island of Iona offers visitors the chance to spend a week living in community with others.

Website   www.iona.org.uk

You will need   • An empty wooden fruit crate from your local greengrocer to
                  make a cradle
                • Pieces of brown hessian and some strips of white cloth to line
                  the cradle
                • Brightly coloured material cut into strips about 15 inches
                  long and 2 inches wide – at least one for each person
                  (If you like, words of welcome can be written on some of the
                  strips)
                • Enough service sheets for everyone

Preparation   Line the cradle with hessian and white cloth and place in the
                middle of the worship space.
                Place the strips of cloth in a pile beside the crate.

The virgin will be with child and will give birth to a son, and they will call him Immanuel – which means 'God with us'.

Matthew 1.23

Welcome   Welcome to this Evening Prayer to celebrate Advent. We are borrowing an idea from the Wild Goose Resource Group, Iona Community, which uses 'clothing of the cradle' in readiness for the birth of Christ as a way of preparing ourselves for Christmas.

Opening   We meet together with one purpose
Responses   **To prepare a place for Jesus.**
                 We do not know the day or the time
                 But we will be ready with open hearts.
                 Let us make a welcome here
                 Let us make a welcome for Jesus.

Song   **Behold, the Saviour of the nations**
                 (*Complete Anglican Hymns Old and New*)
                 OR
                 Keep on looking
                 (*Veni Emmanuel*)

Opening Prayer   Lord Jesus, we have gathered in this place to prepare our hearts and minds to welcome you once more into our lives. We come with our joys and our sorrows. We come with our prayer that this Advent your birth might herald the peace on earth which you will for all people and for which we long.
                 Amen

NT Canticle   **Magnificat (My soul proclaims)**
                 (*Laudate*)
                 OR
                 Magnificat (Canon)
                 (Songs from *Taizé*)

Reading   **Matthew 1.18–25**

Song	**For Mary, mother of our Lord** (*Hymns Old and New: One church, one faith, one Lord*) OR **No wind at the window** (*Innkeepers and Light Sleepers*)
Invitation to Commitment	As we approach Christmas, we buy presents in preparation to give to our friends and neighbours. But how can we prepare to welcome Jesus who is at the heart of the season? We may begin to think about that now, by joining in a very simple action. In front of us is a crate which, if covered with cloth, might make a fine cradle for a baby. Beside the crate are strips of cloth which, if laid on top of each other, might make a patch-work quilt on which a baby could be laid. So let us be still for a moment and turn our minds away from preparing for Christmas, to preparing for Jesus.
Silence	*This will last about 10 minutes* While we sing the song we may, as and when we wish, come forward to lay strips of cloth across the cradle symbolizing our intention to make a place and keep a welcome for Jesus. (Words adapted from *Cloth for the Cradle* and used with permission © Wild Goose Resource Group, Wild Goose Publications, 1997)

Weaving of the Cloth

Song	**Cloth for the cradle** (*Cloth for the Cradle*)
Prayers	Here is a place for you, Lord Jesus. **Just as our hands have made it ready,** **so make our hearts ready** **to love and to welcome you.** **Be born again,** **not in a manger,** **but in us.**

Make us your Bethlehem,
where God is personal
and all things and all people
are made new.
Amen

(Words from *Cloth for the Cradle* used with permission © Wild
Goose Resource Group, Wild Goose Publications, 1997)

Song

O, comfort my people
(*Laudate*)
OR
When our God came to earth
(*Hymns Old and New: One church, one faith, one Lord*)

Blessing

**May God bless us this Advent
and find us ready and prepared
to welcome Jesus.
Amen**
Let us go from this place in peace and hope.
Thanks be to God.

AFTER A NATURAL DISASTER

This service was used after the tsunami in South Asia, when a small group got together for half an hour one Sunday evening just to be quiet and reflect together on what had happened. A picture from the press was chosen as an 'icon' which was used as the focus for the prayers. It was the picture of a young dead girl's hand sticking out of the sand. Using contemporary pictures is one way of giving a focal point to a service. This Evening Prayer shows you how this particular picture was used as a response to the tsunami. It may help you in responding to another disaster.

You will need
- Either 20 or 32 white tiles
- Thick black marker pens to write on the tiles
- Nightlights in a basket
- A specific picture from the press, illustrating the disaster, which can be presented as a PowerPoint presentation or mounted on an easel
- CD player and CD of suitable music
- Service sheets for everyone

Preparation

As this is more of a time of reflection than a service the setting should be a small space where everyone can be together.

Lay the tiles on the floor in the shape of a cross.

Write the names of the people, or places involved in the disaster, on the tiles in large bold letters – put a few lighted candles on the cross.

Place the basket of nightlights and the pens next to the cross.

Arrange the chairs around the cross and in view of the picture.
Keep the lights low and have music playing quietly when people arrive.

To this day, we know, the entire creation sighs and throbs with pain . . .

Romans 8.23

Welcome

We have come here tonight to allow ourselves some time to be still and reflect upon what has been happening in South Asia during the past week.

It has been so overwhelming for us just seeing the images on the television and in our papers. Yet we are so far away. What it has been like for those there we cannot begin to imagine. We will use our time together to pray, sing, reflect and join together in our human sadness, as part of the communion of saints here on earth.

We have selected one image from the press, which we will use as an 'icon' in our intercessions later in the service. It is very shocking, but perhaps we can use it to draw us into a deeper perspective on these things. During the silence particularly you might like to reflect upon the image. We are told it is a hand belonging to a young girl. We do not know her name, but her name is known to God. She is one of the 300,000 people who have died – each one an individual like this young girl, and each one a precious child of God.

Song

Do not be afraid (verses 1 and 2)
(*Hymns Old and New: New Anglican Edition*)

Reading

Romans 8.20–23 read from *The Epistle of Paul to the Romans* (C. H. Dodd)

Creation was not rendered futile by its own choice, but by the will of him who thus made it subject, the hope being that creation as well as humanity would one day be freed from its thraldom to decay and gain the glorious freedom of the children of God. To this day we know, the entire creation sighs and throbs with pain; and not only so, but even we ourselves, who have the Spirit as a foretaste of the future, even we sigh to ourselves as we wait for the redemption of the body.

Psalm 46   *Say alternate verses*

Reading   **Revelation 21.1–5**

Quiet reflective music

Silence   *This will last for about 10 minutes*

Lighting candles *At the end of the silence we are invited to take one or more nightlights and place them on the names on the tile cross. We may have other names to add. Our prayer is that God's light will shine in these dark times and make the way easier for those who are involved in the disaster*

Prayer   *Before and between each intercession we shall sing*
Do not be afraid, for I have redeemed you.
I have called you by your name;
You are mine.

A hand,
A young girl's hand
A dead young girl's hand
We do not know her name, but her family does, and God does
She is . . .
Someone's daughter
Someone's sister
Someone's aunt
Someone's cousin
Someone's friend . . .
Father, enable her family to know your love for them as they grieve for their precious child . . .

Lord, hear our prayer
And let our cry be heard by you.
Sung response

Who gave the girl her bracelet?
Was it her birthday present?
Was it made by her school friend as a friendship bracelet?
Was it brightly coloured to reflect her life of fun and laughter?
Father, thank you for her life, her laughter, her fun.
May her friends be aware of being held in your loving embrace, as they now have to live on without her laughter around them.
May the communities which have been ripped apart, the parents without children, the children without parents, and the friends now gone, know your comfort and love.

Lord, hear our prayer
And let our cry be heard by you.
Sung response

Is the hand crying out 'help me'?
Or is the hand crying out 'help them'?
Is it pointing us towards those left behind?
Is it pointing us to those who now have to build a new life?
Is it requesting us to be aware of the family of the world, of which we are all part?
We know we are all part of the body of Christ here on earth, so if one part is hurting we should all be hurting.
Father, we pray that we will respond generously to the situation that our sisters and brothers in South Asia find themselves in, not just today but in the months and years to come.

Lord, hear our prayer
And let our cry be heard by you.
Sung response

Is the hand reaching out to hold the hand of God?
Is it a message to us to put our trust in God?

To let God lead us onwards into the dark places on earth and trust that he will shine his Glorious Light to show us the way, both here on earth and onwards into the life to come?

Lord, hear our prayer
And let our cry be heard by you.
Sung response

The Lord's Prayer

Let us say the prayer that is said by Christians throughout the world, the prayer that Jesus taught us:

Our Father in heaven . . .

Reflection

I said to the man who stood at the gate of the year
(Minnie Louise Haskin 1875–1957)

**I said to the man who stood at the gate of the year,
'Give me a light that I may tread safely into the unknown.'
And he replied, 'Go out into the darkness and put your hand into the hand of God, that shall be to you better than a light and safer than a known way.'
So I went forth and, finding the hand of God, trod gladly into the night.
He led me towards the hills and the breaking of day in the lone east.**

Everyone leaves quietly in their own time

ALL SAINTS

You will need
- Separate slips of paper with sentences describing saints, eg:
  Saints are people who make Christ known
  Saints can be ordinary people like you and me
  Saints are people who inspire us – people who are no longer alive and also people who are alive today
  We are all part of the Communion of Saints
  Saints lead us on a right path
  Saints shine with the Light of Christ, and so on . . .
- Pictures of saints or names of saints on cards
- A large candle and a selection of other candles
- A sand tray and a basket of nightlights
- CD player
- CD of *God Beyond All Names* by Bernadette Farrell
- Service sheets for everyone

Preparation
The candles are lit and arranged at the front of the worship space around the pictures or name cards.
The sand tray and basket of nightlights are placed on a table nearby.
Choose people to read the sentences about saints.

Blessed are the pure in heart, for they will see God.

Matthew 5.8

Welcome
Welcome to our Evening Prayer. Tonight we are thinking about saints. We celebrate certain saints' feast days during the year, but at All Saints' Tide we think about saints more

generally and give thanks for their witness to God and their inspiration in our lives. It is a time of light and thanksgiving. The 'saints' we remember at this time are not only saints of old, but also saints in our families and communities who show us the Light of Christ by the way they live and the example of love that they set.

Song	**Gracious God, in adoration** (*New Start Hymns and Songs*) OR **As we are gathered** (*Hymns Old and New: One church, one faith, one Lord*)
Responses	With the saints, we are called to worship **All are welcome here.** With the saints, we give thanks for God's goodness **Holy is God's name.** With the saints, we bring our hopes and our fears **We will listen to the word of God.**
Reading	Colossians 1.1–14
Song	**Will you come and follow me** (*Common Praise*) OR **Living God, your word has called us** (*New Start Hymns and Songs*)
Reading	Matthew 5.1–12
Who are saints?	Who are saints? Let's listen . . . *The people who have been given slips of paper speak up from where they are sitting*
Music	**Saints of God in Glory** (Bernadette Farrell) *As we listen to this song we may come forward to light candles for those people who have inspired us*

Prayers

For the saints of old who responded to your call to spread the good news of love and joy and peace
Lord, we give you thanks.

For the courage they showed in the face of danger and for their lives laid down for our sake
Lord, we give you thanks.

For saints among us today, for their inspiration and teaching
Lord, we give you thanks.

For the hidden saints, those who do your work quietly and without acclaim
Lord, we give you thanks.

For future saints, that they may grow in the knowledge of your kingdom
Lord, we give your thanks.

Song

You are called to tell the story
(*Laudate*)
OR
We are called to stand together
(*Sing Glory*)

The Blessing

May we follow in the Way of the saints
May we listen to the Truth that they speak
May we live the Life that God would have us live,
and may the blessing of God the Father, God the Son, and God the Holy Spirit be with us this night and always.
Amen

ALL SOULS

we remember them

A few weeks before the service send out an invitation to everyone in the parish who has had someone die in the past few years. This service is an excellent opportunity to reach out to those in the parish who might not know about All Souls Day, and therefore might not think about coming to the service. After the service serve refreshments and make the visitors welcome.

You will need
- A list of names of those being remembered. The names need to be collected in the weeks before the service, or as people arrive at the door, or look up the names of those who have died in the parish in the past year. These are to read out during the service
- Autumn leaves that have been dried flat, or photocopy and cut out paper leaves using the template at the back of the book, page 172
- Felt pens to write on the leaves
- Three printed copies of 'The Leaves' for three voices to read
- A basket of spring bulbs, enough for everyone at the service
- CD player
- CD of Barber's *Adagio for Strings*
- Candles and nightlights
- Service sheets for everyone

Preparation   This is a quiet service which will work with either a few peo-
                   ple or a larger gathering. If only a few people come, sit
                   together around a focal point. If it is a larger gathering, sit in
                   the main body of the church encouraging people to sit
                   together.

                   As people arrive give them a dried leaf or paper leaf and a
                   pen. They take these to their seats. Invite them to write the
                   name or names of those who have died, whom they are
                   remembering, onto the leaves.

                   Ask several people to read out the list of names of those who
                   have died.

                   Ask three people to read the passage from 'The Leaves'.

                   Arrange a focal point at the altar, with candles and flowers
                   and the basket of bulbs.

**For everything there is a season, and a time for every matter under heaven:
a time to be born, and a time to die; a time to plant, and a time to pluck up
what is planted.**

Ecclesiastes 3

Welcome   We have come here tonight to remember those who have died,
                   and to give thanks for their lives and for how they were woven
                   with ours. We acknowledge the pain of being the ones left
                   behind, but also acknowledge their going on to being closer to
                   God. We might like to write the names of those who have died
                   on the dried leaves we have been given. Without death there is
                   no resurrection, without autumn and winter there is no spring.
                   Later on in the service we are invited to throw down the leaves
                   and pick up a bulb. Although the bulb, like the leaves, now
                   looks dried and dead, it holds inside it the potential for new life
                   in the form of a flower.

Song   Lord, we pray, be near us
                  Tune Cranham 65 65 D

1   Lord, we pray, be near us,
    In this time of grief;
    Bring us peace and healing,
    Solace and relief:
    Heaviness surrounds us
    Like a storm-filled cloud;
    Sounds of day and sunlight
    Now seem harsh and loud.

2   As the shadows deepen
    Chasing out the light;
    Hold us in your hand, and
    Lead us through the night:
    May we, in our sorrow,
    Feel your loving care;
    When life overwhelms us
    Know that you are near.

3   In the end we trust that
    All shall be made well;
    Send your Holy Spirit
    In our hearts to dwell:
    Gently, oh so gently,
    Day must dawn again;
    Shafts of golden sunlight
    Shining through the rain.
                  Text © Jan Brind 2004

Reading   The Leaves (Adapted from *Bambi* by Felix Saltern)
                  The leaves were falling from the trees. Two leaves clung on. 'It
                  isn't the way it used to be,' said one leaf to the other.
                  'No, so many of us have fallen off tonight, we're almost the
                  only two left on this branch,' answered the other.
                  'Even when it is warm and the sun shines, a storm or a cloud

burst would come sometimes, and many leaves would be torn off, though they were still young. You never know who is going to go next.'

'The sun seldom shines now,' sighed the second leaf. 'Soon we will go. Can it be true that we are replaced by others, and then when they have gone by others, more and more?'

'It is really true,' whispered the other leaf. 'It makes me feel very sad. Why must we all fall? What happens to us once we have fallen?'

'We sink down . . . what do you think is under us?'

'I don't know, some say one thing, and some another, but nobody knows. No one has ever come back to tell us about it.'

'Which of us will go first?'

'Let's not worry about that now, let's remember how beautiful it was, how wonderful when the sun came out and shone so warmly that we thought we'd burst with life. Do you remember?'

'Yes, I remember, but look at me now. I am so yellow and ugly.'

'No, you are as lovely as the day that you were born.'

Hours passed, a moist wind blew cold and hostile through the branches.

The leaves were torn from their places and spun downwards . . . winter had come.

Song	**O Christ, you wept**
	(*When Grief Is Raw*)
	OR
	Christ's is the world (a touching place)
	(*Hymns Old and New: New Anglican Edition*)

| Reading | Ecclesiastes 3.1–8 |

| Time of quiet reflection | *Use a quiet piece of music. Barber's* Adagio for Strings *is good. It lasts for nearly 10 minutes and can continue to play as the names are read out. Put it on 'repeat' in case you need longer. After a few minutes, start to read out the names. Do not hurry this. Read them in blocks using different voices, placed in* |

*different parts of the church. After all the names have been
read, invite anyone who has a name that is not on the list to
mention the name out loud.*

*Everyone is now invited to come to the focal point or altar to
throw down their leaf, and then collect a spring bulb*

Reading   John 14.1–6
Or   **We can shed tears that they have gone (Anon)**
                 We can shed tears that they have gone
                 or we can smile that they have lived.
                 We can close our eyes and pray that they will come back
                 or we can open our eyes and see all the good that they have
                 left us.
                 Our hearts can be empty because we cannot see them
                 or our hearts can be full with the love that we've shared.
                 We can turn our backs on tomorrow and live yesterday
                 or we can be happy for tomorrow, *because* of yesterday.
                 We can remember them and only that they have gone
                 or we can cherish their memory and let it live on.
                 We can cry and close our minds, be empty and turn our backs
                 or we can do what they would have wanted:
                 smile, open our eyes, love and go on.

Prayers   Do not be afraid for I shall be with you.
                 Lighten our path, Lord, and show us the way.

                 The road ahead can seem very long and very dark after the
                 death of a loved one. Often there seems little point in going on.
                 Sometimes the pain and loss can be quite overwhelming.
                 But God says:
                 Do not be afraid for I shall be with you.
                 Pause
                 Lighten our path, Lord, and show us the way.

                 We hold out to God all those who are here tonight.
                 All those who are newly bereaved, and all those who have
                 journeyed on awhile since their bereavement. May those who

have passed this way, reach out and reassure those who cannot believe the pain and sadness will ever pass.
Do not be afraid for I shall be with you.
Pause
Lighten our path, Lord, and show us the way.

We hold out to God all those here tonight who have seen division in their family since someone has died. May God's way of love heal the hurt and bring the family closer together again.
Do not be afraid for I shall be with you.
Pause
Lighten our path, Lord, and show us the way.

We hold out to God all those here tonight who are remembering their parents. We thank God for the life they gave us.
Do not be afraid for I shall be with you.
Pause
Lighten our path, Lord, and show us the way.

We hold out to God all those here tonight who are remembering children who have died. We expect our children to be our future and when they die so many of our hopes and expectations go with them.
Do not be afraid for I shall be with you.
Pause
Lighten our path, Lord, and show us the way.

We hold out to God all those here tonight who have had their partners die. Those who feel lonely and unsettled, those who long for another human's touch, a hug, a kiss.
Do not be afraid for I shall be with you.
Pause
Lighten our path, Lord, and show us the way.

May all of us here tonight be aware of our neighbours and friends who grieve. May we welcome them into our homes and dare to walk the road with them for a while. May they in time find a new and healed way forward with God at their side.

Do not be afraid for I shall be with you.
Pause
Lighten our path, Lord, and show us the way that we may go on, trusting that God is here with us wherever our path goes.

Prayer　　We say the prayer that Jesus taught us: **Our Father in heaven . . .**

Song　　**Now the green blade riseth**
(*Hymns Old and New: New Anglican Edition*)
OR
Word that formed creation
(*Resurrexit*)

Blessing　　May God's blessing be upon all who gather here tonight
May God's blessing be upon all who grieve
May God's blessing be upon us all, as we journey through life,
　　in times of sadness and in our times of laughter
Let us go out into the world
Let us live our lives well
And let us not be afraid
Go in the peace of the Lord.
Amen

Refreshment

BAPTISM

You will need
- CD player
- CD of Grieg's 'Morning' from *Peer Gynt Suite No.1*
- The large Easter/Paschal candle
- A candle for everyone, with a drip shield, to be given out on arrival
- Small nightlights and candles
- A large bowl and a jug of water on a low table, with a towel
- Service sheets for everyone

Preparation
If possible set the chairs in a half-circle focused on the candles, the large Easter candle and the bowl and jug of water. There are several prayers and a reading in this service – ask different people to lead the prayers so there is more than one leader, and the group of people who have gathered together share the leading of the service.
Before the service starts ask someone to light the candle and pour the water when indicated in the service.

> And a voice came from heaven,
> 'You are my Son, the Beloved; with you I am well pleased.'
>
> Mark 1.11

Welcome
Welcome. The theme this evening is baptism – looking at both the baptism of Jesus and our own baptism. The story of what happened at Jesus' baptism is very much the story of what could and should happen at ours. God looks on and says, 'You are my own dear child, I am very pleased with you.' How won-

derful and how scary that is. Wonderful that God thinks we are 'dear' and 'pleasing', and scary that we should have to try to live up to God's expectations of us. At our baptism we are saying that we want to try to live as God's children and we want to be part of God's way. But sticking to the way that God wants, and hopes, we will live is not always easy. So tonight we will reflect on what was said at our baptism and turn again to Christ.

Prayer   *Taken from the* Common Worship Service of Holy Baptism

Our Lord Jesus Christ has told us
that to enter the kingdom of heaven
we must be born again of water and the Spirit,
and has given us baptism as the sign and seal of this new birth.
Here we are washed by the Holy Spirit and made clean.
Here we are clothed with Christ,
dying to sin that we may live his risen life.
As children of God, we have a new dignity
and God calls us to fullness of life.
Amen

Song   **The Lord is my light**
(*Songs and Prayers from Taizé*)
OR
The Lord is my light
(*I Will Not Sing Alone*)

Reading   Mark 1.9–11
Please turn to face the reader

Song   **Do not be afraid**
(*Hymns Old and New: One church, one faith, one Lord*)
OR
My soul is thirsting
(*Go Before Us*)

Prayer   *Adapted from the* Common Worship Service of Holy Baptism

In baptism, God calls us out of darkness into his marvellous light.

The Easter candle is lit

To follow Christ means dying to sin and rising to new life with him.
We are washed clean and can start again.

The water is poured into the bowl

Therefore I ask:
Do we reject the devil and all rebellion against God?
We reject them.

Do we renounce the deceit and corruption of evil?
We renounce them.

Do we repent of the sins that separate us from God and neighbour?
We repent of them.

Do we turn to Christ as Saviour?
We turn to Christ.

Do we submit to Christ as Lord?
We submit to Christ.

Do we come to Christ, the way, the truth and the life?
We come to Christ.

What we have just said is an enormous statement of our intentions to try to live God's way. So let us take a few moments to reflect on what we have just said.

Music   **'Morning' from** *Peer Gynt Suite No. 1* **(Grieg)**

Silence	*After the music there is a time of silence lasting about 10 minutes*
Action	*After the silence everyone is invited to wash their hands in the bowl of water. This is a symbol of being washed clean by God, and being invited to start again. The individual candles can then be lit from the Easter candle, as a symbol of our intention to 'Shine as a light in the world'*
Prayer	*Adapted from the* Common Worship Service of Holy Baptism

We will not be ashamed to confess the faith of Christ crucified
We will try our best, and with God's help, to fight valiantly as disciples of Christ against sin, the world and the devil, and remain faithful to Christ to the end of our lives.

Song	**Take my life, and let it be** (*Common Praise*) OR **Lord, for the years** (*Common Praise*)
Prayer	*Adapted from the* Common Worship Service of Holy Baptism

God has delivered us from the dominion of darkness
and has given us a place with the saints in light.

We have received the light of Christ
so let us walk in this light all the days of our lives.

We shall go out into the world and shine as God's lights
The Light will light our path and show us the Way.

We in turn will shine it on the pathway of those we meet
and in the dark places of the world.

Go! Shine!
With the help of God we will.

BLESSING

You will need
- CD player
- CD of *Fire of Love* by Margaret Rizza
- CD of *Go Before Us* by Bernadette Farrell
- Additional CD of gentle music
- Book *Life of the Beloved* by Henri Nouwen
- Candles, flowers, an icon, incense or fragrant oil

Preparation

As this is more of a reflection than a service the setting should be in a small space – maybe a side chapel or church room.

Arrange chairs in a circle if possible.

Have a central focus made from flowers, candles and an icon.

Light incense or fragrant oil.

Dim the lights but make sure people can read.

Music can be playing quietly as people assemble.

Have enough song sheets for everyone – include the blessing at the end which is said by all.

As beloved children of God, we are blessed.
Henri Nouwen, *Life of the Beloved*

Welcome

Welcome to this quiet time of song, reflection and silence. We are going to sing, listen and pray together. We are going to think and pray about 'blessing' – what it means, how it feels to be blessed, and how we may find ways of blessing others.

Song

Evening Song
Tune Gonfalon Royal 88 88 LM

1   It is the evening of the day,
The sun has set and gone its way;
Now we are gathered here to pray,
We ask you, Lord, with us to stay.

2   Keep us within your constant sight,
Make safe our sleep throughout this night;
Our darkest thoughts you put to flight
And fill us with your healing light.

3   Our homes will soon in stillness lie,
In valley deep and mountain high;
With shining moon and star-filled sky
Creation sings her lullaby.

4   Bless friends and neighbours gathered here;
Bless those we love and hold most dear;
Bless those whose joys and pains we share;
That we may know your presence near.
Amen

Text © Jan Brind 2004

Introduction

Blessing is biblical. We read in Genesis 1 that God created male and female and blessed them. Later, Psalm 34 begins 'I will bless the Lord at all times, God's praise always on my lips' or, in Psalm 128, 'Blessed are all who fear the Lord, who walk in God's ways. You will eat the fruit of your labour, blessings and prosperity will be yours'. In the New Testament in Matthew 5 we have the Sermon on the Mount (known also as the Beatitudes). Jesus taught the people 'Blessed are the poor in spirit, for theirs is the kingdom of God'. Later, Jesus took a loaf of bread and, after blessing it, he broke it, and gave it to his disciples (Matthew 26.26). Some translations of the Bible use the words 'gave thanks' instead of 'blessed'.

Clearly 'blessing' and 'being blessed' are good things. And being blessed can also be closely linked with being broken and given. Just as with the communion bread, each one of us is chosen and blessed by God, and then 'broken' in order to be 'given' to others.

So what is this blessing? And how, in our brokenness, can we use it today?

Our blessing is a gift from God – given to us that we might use it to do God's work. As followers of Jesus Christ, we wish goodness, or God's 'blessing', on all whom we love. We are also challenged to ask for God's blessing on those whom we find difficult! We can 'bless' each other at any time, wanting the best for the other, and this is good – (and not to be confused with the blessing that is bestowed on us by an ordained minister at the end of a service, which is given with the authority of the church, and is a liturgical 'rite').

We can be a 'blessing' to each other in the things that we do and the ways in which we behave. Our 'blessedness' makes it possible for us to see the broken body of Christ in our midst. Our 'blessedness' gives us the responsibility and power to bring healing where there is pain – justice where there is wrongdoing. When we are blessed by others we feel warm inside and cherished. We need to remember that others will feel this when we bless them.

Song

Be still and know that I am God
(*Hymns Old and New: One church, one faith, one Lord*)
OR
O, the love of my Lord
(*Be Still and Know*)

Who, apart from the Lord, blesses us today? After we have listened to words taken from *Life of the Beloved* by Henri Nouwen, we will hear the words of a Gaelic blessing adapted by Margaret Rizza to music composed by her and then there will be a period of silence lasting about 10 minutes as we reflect and give thanks for the people in our lives who make us feel blessed.

Reading	From **Life of the Beloved** (Henri Nouwen)

(Being present) can allow us to see how many blessings there are for us to receive: the blessings of the poor who stop us on the road, the blessings of the blossoming trees and fresh flowers that tell us about new life, the blessings of music, painting, sculpture and architecture – all of that – but most of all the blessings that come to us through words of gratitude, encouragement, affection and love. These many blessings do not have to be invented. They are there, surrounding us on all sides. But we have to be present to them and receive them. They don't force themselves on us. They are gentle reminders of that beautiful, strong, but hidden, voice of the one who calls us by name and speaks good things about us.

Music	**A Blessing** (Margaret Rizza)

Silence	

Song	**Bless the Lord**
	(*Songs from Taizé*)
	OR
	Open our eyes, Lord
	(*Be Still and Know*)

Whom do we bless? After we have listened to a reading from the first letter of Peter we will hear music and words composed by Bernadette Farrell and then there will be a period of silence lasting about 10 minutes as we reflect and consider the people in our lives who may be encouraged by a blessing from us.

Reading	1 Peter 3.8–12

Music	**The Face of Christ** (Bernadette Farrell)

Silence	

Reading	**Alternative Beatitudes** (Anon)

Blessed are you who do not shun me
but embrace me as I struggle to find the gift within the pain.
Blessed are you who do not shrink from sharing
that you too have known the searing cloud.
Blessed are you who listen
and by listening affirm me as I am.
Blessed are you to tell me I am precious
and worthy of the deepest cherishing.
Blessed are you who fan the tiny flame
that shines more brightly in the dark.
Blessed are you who know me as I am.

Prayer	**Song of Prayer** (*Crafts for Creative Worship*) OR **One is the body** (*Hymns Old and New: One church, one faith, one Lord*)

Blessing	**May the blessing and peace of God** **be with us all this night** **and in the days to come.** **Amen**

CELEBRATING COMMUNITY

You will need
- A basket of heart-shaped biscuits
- CD player
- CD of *The Song and the Silence* by Marty Haugen
- Cut out paper people, each with a small piece of double sided sticky tape on the back, and a pen, for each person
- A large sheet of paper mounted on a board, with the words 'All of you are Christ's body and each one is a part of it' written in large letters in the centre
- Service sheets for everyone

Preparation
Have the large sheet of paper placed centrally so that the paper people can be stuck onto it. Display this as the focal point.
Arrange the chairs in a horseshoe-shape looking towards the focal point.

All of you are Christ's body, and each one is a part of it.
1 Corinthians 12.27

Welcome
This evening we are gathered here together to reflect upon and celebrate our community in its broadest sense – our families both at home and in the church, the communities we live in, the communities we work with and our friends near and far. Together we all make up the body of Christ. Everyone is as important as each other, each bringing their own unique gifts, all precious in God's sight.

Song	**Brother, sister, let me serve you** (*Common Praise*) OR **Let love be real** (*Hymns Old and New: One church, one faith, one Lord*)
Opening responses	We come here tonight to seek the love of God in this community. **Let us leave tonight with God's Spirit entwining us together.** We pray tonight that we will see each other as God's precious children. **And recognize the gifts we are each given to be used to God's glory as his body here on earth.**
Prayer	*Adapted from the prayer by St Teresa of Avila* Christ has no body now on earth, **But ours.** No hands **But ours.** No feet **But ours.** Ours are the eyes **with which he looks with compassion on the world.** Ours are the feet **by which he can go about doing good.** And ours **are the hands by which others will be blessed and comforted.** **Amen**
Reading	1 Corinthians 12.12–27
Speaking to your neighbour	*Invite everyone to turn to their neighbour and exchange names and where they come from. Ask them to tell each other about one gift they have which contributes to the greater good of their community. This could include making coffee, welcoming people into their homes, leading worship, caring for*

children, visiting a friend – the list is endless. After this invite each person to write their neighbour's name and one of their gifts onto a paper person. Everyone now gets up and sticks their paper person onto the large sheet of paper at the front. Try to stick them in a circle so they are 'holding hands'

Song   *Standing in a large circle everyone should now hold hands and sing the prayer that Jesus taught us,* The Lord's Prayer

              Father God in heaven
              (*Praise God Together*)

Song   **God's Spirit is in my heart**
              (*Hymns Old and New: New Anglican Edition*)
              OR
              Community of Christ
              (*Go Before Us*)

              Everyone now returns to their place and sits or kneels

Recorded Music   **Gathered in the love of Christ/Canon in D** (Marty Haugen)

Silence   *There is now 10 minutes of silence. At the end of the silence a basket of heart-shaped biscuits is passed around and everyone takes one. These biscuits are to be taken away and given to someone in your community who needs to know that God loves them*

Prayers   We thank you, God, for the millions of gifts that you give to each one of us.
              May we use them to your glory.

              We thank you, God, for our many communities: family, church, workplace, clubs, school . . . We pray we will be bearers of your light to each group we are involved in.
              May we shine as a light in your world.

We pray for the many communities that are broken and fragmented by hatred and disharmony especially . . .
May we bring your peace.

We hold out to God all those who are not aware of being a member of any community because of isolation and loneliness.
May we bring your love to them.

We hold out to God all those who are in our community but who we would prefer not to notice, or who we would prefer not to be there.
May our eyes be opened to see them as our fellow brothers and sisters and as God's precious children.

We thank God for this community gathered here tonight and for the many gifts we have between us. We pray we will use them to the glory of God.
Amen

Song
Let there be love
(*Celebration Hymnal for Everyone*)
OR
God of mission, still you send us
(*New Start Hymns and Songs*)

Going out
Let us go out into our communities in peace and love and hope and joy.
In the name of Christ
Amen.

Refreshment may now be served, so that everyone has the opportunity to meet the people in their community. More heart-shaped biscuits can be served.

CHRISTIAN UNITY

It is always good for local churches to get together to celebrate ecumenically. A joint evening service, either preceded or followed by coffee and biscuits, gives Christians of different denominations a chance to meet each other. Many deaneries hold a service of this kind in a different church each year.

The following service follows closely the pattern of an Evening Prayer at the Taizé Community in Burgundy, France. The Community numbers both Protestant and Catholic brothers among its number. Its work with young adults from all over the world speaks of peace and reconciliation – of a 'trust on earth'.

Website
: www.taize.fr
Find out more about Taizé and, in particular, its ministry to young adults from this excellent website

You will need
- A focus – either an icon of the cross or other icon, or a large lit candle, or an open Bible
- One unlit candle and a taper
- Flowers and greenery to decorate
- Cushions, rugs and prayer stools if you have them so that some people can sit on the floor if they want to
- Lots of candles in holders – nightlights work well
- Incense is usual – or fragrant oil
- CD player
- CDs of quiet music to play as people arrive and leave – there are many CDs recorded at Taizé (try *Laudate Omnes Gentes* or *Taizé Instrumental*)
- Someone to lead the singing if there is no accompanying music group – tuning forks are useful – or one of the above mentioned CDs to use as an accompaniment

- Service sheets and music sheets for everyone
- For this service you will need a loaf of bread in a basket
  All the songs in this service are chosen from the books *Songs from Taizé* and *Taizé: Songs for Prayer*

Preparation   If you have chairs try to arrange them in a semi-circle around the focus – arrange rugs, cushions and prayer stools.
Light the candles and incense or fragrant oil.
Place the bread basket in front of the focus.
Dim the lights – but make sure that service sheets and music can be read.
Play gentle music as people are arriving.

You are the people of God; he loved you and chose you for his own.

Colossians 3.12

Welcome   Welcome to this time of quiet prayer and reflection. We shall be using a pattern of worship from the ecumenical Community of Reconciliation in Taizé, France. The songs are simple, using phrases taken from the Bible, which are sung repeatedly. As we sing the words to the songs in this way we may find that our songs become prayers and that we are being brought closer to Christ. An 'Amen' signifies the end of each song. There will be a time of silence lasting about 10 minutes. At the end of the silence we will share a loaf of bread. As Jesus taught us, though we are many, we are one body, because we all share in one bread.

Song   **Laudate Dominum (Sing, praise and bless the Lord)**
OR
In the Lord

Song   **The kingdom of God**
OR
Stay with us

Psalm	**Psalm 33.1–12** *This may be said responsively*
Song of Light	**With you, O Lord** OR **Within our darkest night** *During this song ask someone to come forward to light the unlit candle. This is to show that the light of Christ is always with us*
Reading	**Colossians 3.12–17** *Everyone turns to face the reader*

The Lord's Prayer

| Intercessions | *Between each prayer sing a response such as **Kyrie 12** or **Ubi caritas** and involve different people in the reading of the prayers*

For the people of our churches gathered here this evening, that we may celebrate our faith together, embracing all that we share, and acknowledging our diversity
Lord, we pray.
Sung response

For those who are yet to discover the love and community that is to be found in the fellowship of the church
Lord, we pray.
Sung response

For those of other faiths, that we may seek to understand and learn from each other
Lord, we pray.
Sung response |

For those in pain or distress this night, and for those who are lonely, that we may find ways of bringing love and companionship into their lives
Lord, we pray.
Sung response

For this troubled world, that we may have courage to stand by what is right, and that we may act together swiftly to bring about justice and peace for all people
Lord, we pray.
Sung response

For the breaking and sharing of bread, that we may recognize that we are one body in Christ
Lord, we pray.
Sung response

Silence   *If you like, play some gentle music appropriate to the theme to help people settle into the silence. After the silence the basket of bread is passed around*

Song   **God is forgiveness**
OR
O Christe Domine Jesu

Song   **Sing to God**
OR
Praise our God

Song   **Gloria, gloria (Canon)**
OR
Jubilate Deo (Canon)

If you have had refreshments at the beginning of the service, or if they are in a different room, allow people to stay quietly until they feel ready to leave

COST OF DISCIPLESHIP

You will need
- A large cross
- A large fireproof container to burn pieces of paper in and some matches
- 'Bank of God the Almighty' £10 money notes – one for each person. Photocopy the banknote template at the back of the book, page 173
- Pencils for everyone
- CD player
- CD of *God Beyond All Names* by Bernadette Farrell
- Candles

Preparation

Lay out the worship space focused around the cross.
Place the bowl and matches on a small table by the cross.
Give everyone a '£10 note' and a pencil.
Have enough service sheets for everyone.

'If any want to become my followers, let them deny themselves and take up their cross daily and follow me'.

Luke 9.23

'Just as you did it to one of the least of these who are members of my family, you did it for me!'

Matthew 25.40

Welcome	This evening we are gathered here together to reflect upon the cost of our discipleship. What does it cost for us to follow Jesus? Is the cost greater than the gain? Is the cost too high? What do we see as the disadvantages? What are the advantages? Big questions that we don't very often reflect upon. We will use the time to listen to God. To praise God. To be still and know that God is God. Our Lord and King!

Song

Bless the Lord
(*Songs and Prayers from Taizé*)
OR
Come all you people
(*Come All You People*)

Readings

Luke 9.23–25
Matthew 25.31–40

Song

In love you summon
(*There Is One Among Us*)
OR
The Lord is my song
(*Songs and Prayers from Taizé*)

Psalm

Psalm 86
Say together alternate verses

Prayers

Father, I know you said that we should be aware of the hungry and thirsty, that we should feed them and share what we have. But the situation seems so enormous, and what difference would my little bit make to so many? They are so far away, and anyway I have enough to do without taking them all on board as well.
Father, forgive us.

Father, it is all very well saying we should welcome strangers, but they are scary, they sometimes smell, and I don't know if I can trust them – and they might not like the way I do things. So it might be better if I leave that to someone else.
Father, forgive us.

Father, I am sure I would help those who sleep in the streets at night if I were trained. They do look cold and some new clothes might well help. But I wouldn't know what to say to them. I am sure it is better to leave that to the experts.
Father, forgive us.

Father, I sometimes wonder why it is that people abuse their bodies with alcohol and drugs. It makes me wonder if they really should be given treatment, because it is really their fault. They clog up the beds in the hospitals. It really isn't right.
Father, forgive us.

Father, have you heard how comfy prisons are these days? Do you know they even have TVs and radios in their rooms? I'm glad I don't have to go near them.
Father, forgive us.

Sometimes, Lord, it is hard to forget self.
Father, forgive us.

Sometimes it is hard to be different.
Father, forgive us.

Sometimes we get hurt, Lord, and we don't want to be your disciples.
Father, forgive us.

Sometimes we forget you are there always holding us, and we grow weak and helpless, and turn away from you.
Father, forgive us.

Sometimes we do not trust that 'all shall be well'.
Father, forgive us.

Sometimes we forget you said that, if we follow you, we have to take up our cross. You didn't say it would be easy.
Father, forgive us.

But sometimes, Lord, we remember what Life you offer us and that, by following you, we have everything. Help us to love those who are hard to love, to welcome those who are hard to welcome, and to be generous with our many gifts of both time and money. Help us to welcome your love. May your love be the love between us and each person we meet. Help us to shine as lights in your world and to be worthy of being called your disciples.
O Lord, hear our prayer.

Music   **God has chosen me** (Bernadette Farrell)

Silence   *There is now a silence lasting about 10 minutes. We can use this time to reflect on what it means to be Jesus' disciple. What does it cost us? Let us write our thoughts on the back of the 'God money' £10 note*

Action   *Anyone who would like to can take their 'God money' and burn it at the foot of the cross, offering to God our discipleship and praying that we might be worthy to be called disciples of Jesus*

Song   **With you, O Lord**
(Taizé: Songs for Prayer)
OR
Ubi caritas (Living charity)
(Songs and Prayers from Taizé)

EASTER

Here is an evening liturgy based loosely on an Evening Prayer at the ecumenical Community of Reconciliation at Taizé in Burgundy, France. The songs we have chosen are just suggestions and are all taken from Taizé song books. It might be that your congregation knows certain songs from Taizé and, in that case, it would be helpful to plan the liturgy using those songs. It is also perfectly all right to use songs that do not originate from Taizé – the shorter songs for worship from Iona work well. Or mix the two!

Website   www.taizé.fr

You will need
- Small rolls of bread in a basket
- CD player
- CD of *I Will Not Sing Alone* (The Wild Goose Collective and Macappella)
- Icon of the cross or other icon as a focus
- Flowers and greenery
- Paschal candle
- Candles of different sizes
- Incense or fragrant oil and burner
- Rugs, cushions and prayer stools
- Books *Songs from Taizé* and *Songs and Prayers from Taizé*
- Service sheets for everyone

Preparation   Arrange the flowers and greenery around the cross or icon.
Light the Paschal candle and arrange other lit candles.
Place the basket of bread rolls beneath the cross or icon.
If you have chairs try to arrange them in a semi-circle around the focus.
Arrange rugs, cushions and prayer stools.

Light all the candles and incense or fragrant oil.
Dim the lights but make sure that words can be read.
Play gentle music as people arrive.

'It is the Lord!'

John 21.7

Welcome   Welcome to this time of quiet prayer and reflection. We shall
be using a pattern of worship from the ecumenical Community
of Reconciliation in Taizé, France. The songs are simple, using
phrases taken from the Bible, which are sung repeatedly. As we
sing the words to the songs in this way we may find that our
songs become prayers and that we are being brought closer to
Christ. An 'Amen' signifies the end of each song. There will be
a time of silence lasting about 10 minutes.

Song   **Laudate omnes gentes (Sing praises, all you peoples)**

Song   **Lord Jesus Christ**

Poem   **The One Bread** (Jack Osbourn)
They were all together in an upper room
Having supper
They all ate a bit off the same loaf
And the symbolism struck them
'We are a gang of chaps
Separate individuals
But now we have something in common
Because we all contain the same bread'
He said, 'Do this in remembrance of me'
So, whenever they ate bread together,
He would be there
In all their heads simultaneously
Like parted lovers
Both looking at the moon
And holding close – in their minds

He passed round a cup of wine
They all drank from it
One after the other
And the bread and the wine and the cup
Were symbols of unity forever
Why don't you try it?
Perhaps in Lent
It's not just bread and wine you know
There's more to it than that
That's what He meant

© June Osbourn 1996

Reading   **John 21.1–14**

Intercessions   *Between the intercessions sing* **Lord of all goodness**

Lord Jesus Christ, Mary recognized you only when you called
her by name. We thank you that you know us by our names as
individuals; we pray that we may never fail to hear your call.
Lord, we pray.
Sung response

Lord Jesus Christ, Cleopas and his friend recognized you only
when you broke and blessed the bread. We thank you for the
gift of the bread of life broken and shared for us; we pray that
we may never fail to share our daily bread with others.
Lord, we pray.
Sung response

Lord Jesus Christ, Thomas recognized you only when he saw
and touched you. We thank you for the gift of faith by which
we know you; we pray that we may see you with the eye and
heart and mind of faith.
Lord, we pray.
Sung response

Lord Jesus Christ, your disciples did not know you as you
stood on the beach and told them to cast their nets. We thank

you for the gift of your Holy Spirit by which we are strengthened to cast your net over the whole world; we pray for the day when the network of your love will hold all people.
Lord, we pray.
Sung response

Thomas recognized Jesus and said, 'My Lord and my God';
Mary recognized Jesus and called him, 'Rabboni';
John recognized Jesus and said, 'It is the Lord!'
Risen Jesus, may we always know you as our teacher, our Lord and our God.
Lord, we pray
Sung response

The Lord's Prayer

Music	**Jesus Christ, here among us** (Wild Goose Collective and Macappella)
Silence	*There will now be a silence lasting about 10 minutes.* *After the silence a basket of bread rolls will be passed around.* *Please take one home with you to break and share with your family and friends*
Song	**Eat this bread**
Song	**Surrexit Christus (The Lord is risen)**
Song	**Jubilate cœli (Canon) (Heavens, sing with gladness)**

EPIPHANY

You will need
- A doll to represent Jesus lying in a manger
- Book *Imagining God* by Trevor Dennis
- Two readers – one to read the introduction to the story and one to read the story itself
- Small wrapping paper parcels – one for each person. Photocopy the gift wrapping template and follow the instructions at the back of the book, page 174
- Pens
- A basket
- CD player
- CD of instrumental music such as *Icons* by Margaret Rizza or *One Bright Star* by Marty Haugen and Marc Anderson

Preparation

Give everyone a wrapping paper parcel and a pen.
Give everyone a service sheet (or use an OHP).
The atmosphere should be intimate and mysterious – dimmed lights and focus on the manger.

We saw his star in the east and have come to worship him.

Matthew 2.2

Welcome

This evening we gather at the manger to welcome Jesus and, together with the magi, bring to him our gifts. We may not have gold, myrrh or frankincense to offer, but we do have our love and our own words of welcome. We have journeyed a long way since the beginning of Advent, and now the child is born and we are here, and it is our time to worship him.

Song	**A new song God has given** (*Beneath a Travelling Star*) OR **He came down** (*Laudate*)
Opening Responses	We have come to this place to find the Christ child **We have journeyed together from darkness to light.** We have heard the angels sing of peace on earth **Glory to God in the highest.** We have followed a star and bring gifts to Jesus **Let us draw near to welcome him.**
Song	**Holy, holy, holy is the Lord** (*Hymns Old and New: One church, one faith, one Lord*) OR **The Aye Carol** (*Heaven Shall Not Wait*)
Reading	Matthew 2.1–18
Song	**How faint the stable-lantern's light** (*Beneath a Travelling Star*) OR **Like a candle flame (The Candle Song)** (*Sing Glory*)
Story	***A Child Is Born*** (Trevor Dennis)
Song	**O worship the Lord in the beauty of holiness** (*Common Praise*) OR **What shall we give** (*Laudate*)

Silence	*In a time of quiet, while we listen to some music, let us consider what gifts we can offer to Jesus. They might be words of welcome, words of love, words of warning or promises*
Action	*Let us undo our wrapping paper parcels and write down our offerings on the inside. After folding them again we can offer them to Jesus by placing them in the basket at the foot of the manger*

Prayers

For all who are seeking, that they may find you
Jesus, we welcome you.

For your light that shines in our darkness
Jesus, we welcome you.

For the peace you wish for all people
Jesus, we welcome you.

For the message of love that you bring
Jesus, we welcome you.

For your kingdom that it may be found within us
Jesus, we welcome you.

For the wonder and mystery of your birth
Jesus, we welcome you.

Song

Carol at the manger
(*Laudate*)
OR
Lord, the light of your love (Shine, Jesus, shine)
(*Hymns Old and New: One church, one faith, one Lord*)

Blessing

May the love of Jesus surround us
May the joy of Jesus fill our lives
May the hope of Jesus bring us peace
May the light of Jesus continue to guide us on the Way.
Amen

FAMILIES

You will need
- A large vine drawn or painted on a sheet of paper. You can either use a paper table cloth about 5 to 6 ft (1½ to 2 metres) square or you can join three strips of lining paper together to make the background. Draw the vine with a few leaves and bunches of grapes but leave plenty of blank space. Look at the vine illustration at the back of the book, page 175, to see how you might do this.
- A notice board on which to firmly fix the sheet of paper
- Enough sticky labels for everyone – use clip art, or the grapes template (page 176) to decorate each label with a small bunch of grapes leaving enough room for people to write their names (make sure the labels you use can be easily and quickly peeled off their backing)
- Each person will need a service sheet, a sticky label and a felt-tip pen

Preparation
Place the vine at the front of the worship space – everyone should be able to reach some part of it.

Whoever does what my Father in heaven wants him to do is my brother, my sister, and my mother.

Matthew 12.50

Welcome	We gather this evening to celebrate what it means to be 'family'. Not only do we acknowledge and give thanks for members of our own family, but we consider who else might be part of our Christian family. In our baptism liturgy, when we welcome a new member to our church family, we affirm that we are children of the same heavenly Father – the Father who has searched each one of us out, who loves us and who knows us intimately.
Opening Response	We are joined together as one family in God's love and care **Let us thank God in song, prayer and silence.**
Song	**Living God, your word has called us** (*New Start Hymns and Songs*) OR **Let us build a house** (*Hymns Old and New: One church, one faith, one Lord*)
Reading	**1 John 4.7–12**
Song	**O God, you search me (Psalm 139)** (*Laudate*)
Reading	**Matthew 12.46–50**
Silence	*We spend a short time in silence reflecting on who might be members of our own Christian family. These could include not only people whose company we enjoy, but also those who challenge us and make us feel uncomfortable*
Song	**You are the vine** (*Songs of Fellowship*)
Response	We are the family of God **We rejoice that God loves each one of us and calls us by name.**

Action	*We write our names on the labels and bring them forward to stick on the vine – we can also name those whom we consider to be 'members of our family in God'*

Prayers

Let us pray to God our loving Father:

For our families and loved ones
Lord, hear our prayer.

For those in our extended Christian family – those whom we can call mother, brother, sister, and those who challenge us
Lord, hear our prayer.

For those who are alone this night and who long to be held in the warmth and companionship of family life
Lord, hear our prayer.

For those who have been wounded by family breakdown and discord
Lord, hear our prayer.

For loved ones whom we see no longer, but whose names are written on our hearts
Lord, hear our prayer.

For the family of the church here in this place and throughout the world
Lord, hear our prayer.

Song

He's got the whole world in his hand
(*Hymns Old and New: One church, one faith, one Lord*)
OR
Sisters and brothers, with one voice
(*Iona Abbey Music Book*)

Blessing

May God the Father bless our families
May God the Son fill us with love for one another
May God the Holy Spirit lead us in the way of truth.
Amen

HARVEST OF THE BODY OF CHRIST

Here is another evening liturgy based loosely on an Evening Prayer at the ecumenical Community of Reconciliation at Taizé in Burgundy, France. The songs we have chosen are just suggestions and are all taken from Taizé song books. As with all these liturgies please, if you wish, change the songs to ones that are more familiar or that you would prefer to use.

Website   www.taizé.fr

You will need
- An icon of the cross, or other icon, or a large lit candle, or an open Bible
- A large sunflower head at least as big as a dinner plate, with the words 'The Body of Christ in (place)' printed in the middle, drawn on a sheet of card and mounted on an easel (see the sunflower illustration at the end of the book, page 177)
- A large yellow Post-it block from which petal shapes can be cut – the sticky part should be at the base of the petal
- Pens – enough for everyone
- One large unlit candle with taper

- Candles of all sizes, including nightlights
- Flowers and greenery
- Cushions, rugs and prayer stools
- Incense or fragrant oil with a burner
- CD player
- CD of *River of Peace* by Margaret Rizza
- CDs of quiet music to play as people arrive and depart (*Taizé Instrumental* or *Laudate Omnes Gentes* or any CD recorded at Taizé)
- Books – *Songs from Taizé* and *Songs and Prayers from Taizé*
- It is suggested that the Psalm, the Reading and the Lord's Prayer be taken from *The Message* by Eugene H. Peterson
- Service sheets, including music, and a petal shape for everyone

Preparation   If you have chairs try to arrange them in a semi-circle around the focus.
Arrange rugs, cushions and prayer stools.
Light all the candles apart from the one reserved with a taper, and the incense or fragrant oil.
Place the easel at the side but within easy reach of everyone.
Dim the lights but make sure that words can be read.
Play gentle music as people arrive.

Some fell on good earth, and produced a harvest beyond his wildest dreams.
Matthew 13.8

Welcome   Welcome to this time of quiet prayer and reflection. We are celebrating the harvest of ourselves and our gifts as part of the body of Christ. We shall be using a pattern of worship from the ecumenical Community of Reconciliation in Taizé, France. The songs are simple, using phrases taken from the Bible, which are repeated over and over again. As we sing the words to the songs in this way we may find that each song becomes a prayer and that we are being brought closer to Christ. An 'Amen' signifies the end of each song. There will be a time of silence lasting about 10 minutes.

Song	Sing praises all you peoples (Laudate omnes gentes) OR Laudate Dominum (Sing, praise and bless the Lord)
Song	Raise a song of gladness (Jubilate, servite) OR Praise our God
Psalm	Psalm 96.8–13 *The psalm can be read antiphonally, either between the leader and all others, or between men and women*
Song of Light	The Lord is my light OR Our darkness *During this song ask someone to come forward to light the unlit candle. This candle symbolizes the Light of Christ which is always present*
Reading	Matthew 13.1–23

The Lord's Prayer

Intercessions	*Between each prayer sing a response such as **Alleluia** 7 or **We adore you, Lord Jesus Christ** (Adoremus te O Christe)* For we who are gathered in celebration of God's abundant harvest, we give you thanks and pray to the Lord. *Sung response* For families, friends and neighbours, we give you thanks and pray to the Lord. *Sung response* For the gifts we are given that we may discover and use them to your glory, we give you thanks and pray to the Lord. *Sung response* For your beautiful world, that we may be your wise and care-ful stewards, we give you thanks and pray to the Lord. *Sung response* That our brokenness may be the means by which we, together,

become the living and visible body of Christ in this place, we give you thanks and pray to the Lord.

Sung response

For this harvest season that our lives may bring forth the fruit of your Spirit in love and joy and peace, we give you thanks and pray to the Lord.

Sung response

Music   **Creator God** (Margaret Rizza)

Silence   *There is now a period of silence lasting about 10 minutes*

Action   *The sunflower face at the front will not seem complete until we have carefully placed its petals around it. In the same way the body of Christ is not complete until we all work together, using our unique gifts, to bring in God's kingdom in this place. So, as the silence ends, let us write our names on the petals and come forward to place them around the sunflower face*

Song   **Veni Lumen (choral) (Come Holy Spirit, Comforter)**
                OR
                Sing to God

Song   **In the Lord**
                OR
                The Lord is my song (alternative words to O Lord, hear my prayer)

Song   **Magnificat (canon) (Sing out my soul)**
                OR
                Praise our God

At the end of the service play gentle music and don't be in a hurry to tidy up! Allow people to leave in their own time. Serve refreshments

HARVEST OF CREATION

Websites
There are many websites with excellent pictures suitable for this theme of Harvest. Type words such as 'harvest pictures' in the search box. These can be projected onto a screen

You will need
- A selection of candles of varying sizes, including small night-lights
- Conkers – if possible some still in their spiky outer shells
- Various fruits or vegetables – some whole and some split open to show their seeds
- Projector if slides are to be used
- CD player
- CD of *Sacred Weave* by Keith Duke
- A service sheet and a piece of fruit, a vegetable or a conker to give to each person on arrival
- A low table
- Two readers if using 'The Conker'

Preparation
Arrange the chairs in a circle around the table.
Arrange the candles on the table – some in holders so the heights vary.
Arrange the conkers, fruits and vegetables beautifully among the candles.
Have just enough light for people to read comfortably.

What a rich harvest your goodness provides!

Psalm 65.11

Welcome   Tonight we take as our theme the Harvest of Creation. In this service we will give thanks to God for all the good things of his creation: the fruits of the earth which provide for our physical needs. Hidden within these fruits are the seeds of the harvest still to come. Sometimes the hard outer shell has to be broken for the seed to be found. These seeds must die to themselves if they are to be fruitful in the future. And so must we.

Song   **Bless the Lord**
(*Songs from Taizé*)
OR
Unless a grain of wheat
(*Celebration Hymnal for Everyone*)

Reading   **Psalm 65.9–13**

Thanksgiving   *Speak the lines from the following hymn by Fred Pratt Green*
For the fruits of all creation (*Laudate*)

For the fruits of all creation
Thanks be to God;
For these gifts to every nation
Thanks be to God;
For the ploughing, sowing, reaping,
Silent growth while we are sleeping,
Future needs in earth's safe keeping,
Thanks be to God.
In the just reward of labour,
God's will be done;
In the help we give our neighbour,
God's will be done;
In our worldwide task of caring
For the hungry and despairing,
In the harvest we are sharing,
God's will be done.

For the harvests of the Spirit,
Thanks be to God;
For the good we all inherit,
Thanks be to God;
For the wonders that astound us,
For the truths that still confound us,
Most of all, that love has found us,
Thanks be to God.

OR

Reflection

The Conker (*To be read by two voices*)

Look at this spiky shell, so unpromising, so unwelcoming
Hard to get into, leathery, sharp, going brown on the edges,
rotting.
So like us Lord, so hard on the outside, so hard to get into.
Closed with sharp 'keep out' signs all around. Gradually
rotting with our pride and selfishness, slowly dying.
But what a surprise inside!
So smooth, so beautiful, so shiny,
Like mahogany, French polished wood
Nestling in softness, protected.
Could we be full of surprises if you break us open, Lord?
Could we be beautiful if we followed your Way?
As time passes it loses its shine, the beauty goes
It wrinkles and shrivels
It dies.
Do we also need to die, Lord? To die to the many things which
block us from you? That make us lose our beauty and stop us
living as you have intended us to do, full of beauty and life?
Buried. Slowly it splits, the new growth appears
So green, so full of new life, so full of potential.
Lord, we pray you will split us open. Let us be open to your
love so that we will grow again, filled with your new life and
spirit. Help us to be the inside, not the outside, of the conker.
Let us be ready to die, and to burst open again, and to embrace
all that lies before us. Let us be overflowing with your love, full

of the possibilities you offer us. But, Lord, keep your loving protection around us as we try to follow your Way, and become your beautiful people.

This idea could be repeated with other fruits. A sweet chestnut is very spiky on the outside but sweet inside. An artichoke covered with fancy leaves hides an amazing heart. An orange, bright and showy, yet inside so easily broken and shared. The possibilities are endless

Song
Now the green blade riseth
(*Hymns Old and New: New Anglican Version*)
OR
Word that formed creation
(*Resurrexit*)

Reading
From **Song for Sarah** (Paula D'Arcy)

I imagined that I had lived at the time of Christ. How lucky that would have been, I thought . . .
. . . And then it struck me and was so real: Christ *does* live, and we *do* live in the same time. No wishing and no 'if only'.
Christ lives and his Love is here. He alone has never moved. That's the statement of Resurrection. Nothing dies and nothing ends. When we reach one conclusion we only become part of another beginning. Your father wrote it in his Garden Log: 'Every seed has its Easter.' Now finally, I understand.

OR
Matthew 13.18–23

Music
Evening Dedication (Here are my thoughts, Lord)
(*Keith Duke*)

Stillness
A time of silence lasting about 10 minutes
During this time everyone is invited to use the piece of fruit, vegetable or conker that they have been given. Ask them to reflect on the wonder of God's creation, on the need for the

fruit or vegetable to die so that they might live again, and to
think about how God's wish is that we might do the same.
At the end of the silence invite anyone who wishes to share the
thoughts or reflections they have had during the silence.

Song

Now thank we all our God
(*Common Praise* 530)
OR
Thanks be to God
(*Laudate*)

Blessing

May God who created us be delighted with his creation
May we whom God created be filled with God's delights
May we die to ourselves
Live in God's light
And grow in God's Spirit.
Amen

HIV/AIDS

Human Immunodeficiency Virus/Acquired Immune Deficiency Syndrome

HIV/AIDS is a scourge of our times. Apart from natural disaster it is the biggest single threat to the health and well-being of the peoples of the world. Over 38 million people live with HIV/AIDS; 8,000 people die every single day. The disease is devastating large parts of Africa. It is rampant in many other countries. It affects both homosexual and heterosexual people. Mothers with the HIV virus can pass it on to their unborn children. The statistics go on getting worse, not better. There is no cure, although there are anti-retroviral drugs which can hold the symptoms of the disease at bay. Even these drugs are only just becoming available to people in the poorest countries. They are expensive.

But there is a way forward – and it has to do with education and openness. The cause of the spread of the disease is well-documented. We need to unravel the fear that surrounds HIV/AIDS so that we can help, and not isolate, those who suffer.

Websites   Put AIDS into the search box on your computer and you will find a number of relevant websites

You will need
- PowerPoint slide show of pictures interspersed with facts and statistics – these are available on websites – or a display of pictures and fact cards
- A large lit candle on a stand
- Candles and drip shields for everyone
- CD Player
- CD of *Turn My Heart* by Marty Haugen
- Service sheets for everyone
- Refreshments for the end

Preparation	If using PowerPoint set the slide show up so that it is above the focal point and plays continuously or arrange pictures and cards. Place the lit candle to one side. Place chairs in a semi-circle.

Who shall separate us from the love of Christ?

Romans 8.35

Welcome	Welcome to this Evening Prayer. Here is a short liturgy to focus on the tragedy that is HIV/AIDS – and also to help dispel some of the myths. You are welcome to stay for refreshments at the end of the service.
Song	**Christ's is the world** (*Hymns Old and New: One church, one faith, one Lord*) OR **There is a longing** (*Laudate*)
Psalm	**Psalm 41** *Ask two people to read this psalm in blocks alternately*
Reading	**Romans 8.31–39**
Song	**Neither death nor life** (*Gift of God*) OR **We cannot measure** (*Common Praise*)
Music	**Watch, O Lord** (Marty Haugen) *As the music begins two people light their candles from the main candle at the front. They proceed to pass the light to others until all are holding a lighted candle, a symbol that the Light of Christ is always with us overwhelming the darkest places*

Silence	*We remain silent for two or three minutes*
Intercessions	*Between the intercessions we sing*

Lord God, you love us
(*Songs from Taizé*)
OR
Kindle a flame
(*Hymns Old and New: One church, one faith, one Lord*)
We cannot catch AIDS by shaking hands.
Lord, as you reached out with healing hands to those in need, help us to reach out in love to those around us who suffer.
Sung response

We cannot catch AIDS by using the same cup and sharing cutlery.
Lord, as you gathered your disciples around you to share bread in fellowship, let us offer hospitality and a warm welcome to all.
Sung response

We cannot catch AIDS by hugging each other.
Lord, help us to embrace our brothers and sisters in acceptance and compassion.
Sung response

We cannot catch AIDS by being a friend.
Lord, take away our fear that we may walk beside those infected with HIV/AIDS. May we overcome our fear and prejudice by replacing them with knowledge and understanding.
Sung response

At the end of the intercessions the candles are extinguished

Song	**God beyond knowledge**
(*Iona Abbey Music Book*)
OR

If you believe and I believe
(*Hymns Old and New: One church, one faith, one Lord*)

The Peace   **May the love of Christ bring peace and healing**
May the compassion of Christ fill our hearts
May the Spirit of Christ lead us in all wisdom and understanding.
Let us share a sign of peace with each other.

We are invited to stay and meet each other and share refreshment

HOLY WEEK

Each station will need

- Nightlights and candles burning in and among the items being displayed
- Several copies of the Bible text written on card for people to pick up and read
- A large sign with a phrase taken from the Bible reading
- The items illustrating the story
- Chairs, cushions, prayer stools

And at the end

- A CD player
- CD *Sing to God* from the Taizé Community

Station 1   **The story of the Last Supper**

- Cards with Mark 14.22–24 written on them
- A table cloth with a broken loaf of bread in a basket and a jug with wine and a pottery chalice laid out on it
- A card inviting people to take bread and wine
- Items to give the impression of a meal happening, plates, cutlery . . .
- A large sign saying, 'Do this in remembrance of me'

Station 2	**Judas betrays Jesus**

- Cards with Matthew 26.21–25 and 47–50 written on them
- A bag of 'silver' coins spilling out, and a hangman's rope
- A large sign saying, 'Here comes my betrayer'

Station 3	**Jesus prays**

- Cards with Matthew 26.36–41 written on them
- Display of greenery to give the impression of a garden
- Pillows and rugs
- A large sign saying, 'Are you still sleeping?'

Station 4	**Peter denies knowing Jesus**

- Cards with Mark 14.66–72 written on them
- A picture or model of a cockerel and a 'fire' made out of sticks with red coloured paper to make it look as if it is burning
- A large sign saying, 'I do not know the man'

Station 5	**Pilot washes his hands**

- Cards with Matthew 27.22–24 written on them
- A bowl of water and a towel with a sign inviting people to wash their hands
- A large sign saying, 'Crucify him' and 'It is your responsibility'

Station 6	**Jesus is flogged**

- Cards with Matthew 27.28–31 written on them
- A crown made from thorns, a stick and a purple robe
- A large sign saying, 'Hail, King of the Jews!'

Station 7	**Jesus is crucified**

- Cards with Luke 23.34a written on them
- A wooden cross, as large as possible
- A hammer and large nails
- A sign inviting people to hammer a nail into the wood
- A large sign saying, 'Father forgive them, for they do not know what they are doing'

Station 8	**Jesus dies and the temple curtain splits in two**

- Cards with Matthew 27.45 and 50–51 written on them
- Pieces of fabric each with a small tear so they can be torn into two
- A large sign saying, 'The curtain of the temple was torn in two from top to bottom'
- Sign inviting people to tear a piece of fabric into two
- Cards with the words 'Let God's light break through into . . .' (see the template at the end of the book, page 178)
- Pen to write on the cards
- Extra candles to light and place by the cards

Station 9	**Jesus is placed in the tomb**

- Cards with John 19.38–42 written on them
- A large sign saying, 'They laid Jesus there'
- Some white sheets
- Some jars of spices

Preparation	Prepare each 'station' as described, spacing them around the church.

Jesus, remember me when you come into your kingdom.

Luke 23.42

Welcome	Tonight we have come together to spend time reflecting on Jesus' journey from the Last Supper to his death. Our time together will not be structured. The time, about an hour, is there for each person to use in his or her own way. Around the church are places where we can pause and reflect. Some have things to 'do', while others are just places to 'be'. Each one tells a small part of the story. This is written out on cards. At the end of an hour the Taizé song 'Jesus, remember me', will be played. Everyone leaves in silence, scattered, as the disciples were, after the Last Supper.

JOURNEYING

You will need
- A basket of clean stones – small enough to be held but large enough to build a cairn
- Extra stones to make the base of a cairn
- A low table
- CD player
- CD of *Christ, Be Our Light* by Bernadette Farrell
- Service sheets for everyone

Preparation
If possible place chairs in a circle.
In the centre, or at the front, place a low table on which the beginning of a cairn should be built using the extra stones.

'You also, like living stones, are being built into a spiritual house'.
1 Peter 2.5

Welcome
This evening we are looking at 'journeying'. Our whole life is a journey – from the moment we are born, through death and beyond. At different times during our life good things, and sometimes difficult things, happen and many of these remain in our memory as markers. Our faith journey also has its fruitful times and its barren times. Sometimes God feels close. Sometimes God feels far away. God is always saying, 'Do not be afraid – follow me.' God longs for us to say, 'We are not frightened. We will follow you – show us the way.'

Have you ever seen a cairn? A cairn is a pile of stones built as a marker, or a sign – sometimes on the summit of a hill, or to celebrate a holy place. The stones have been put there by pilgrims – or travellers – to let people know that they, too, have passed by that same spot on their journey.

God wants us to be living stones, building God's kingdom, and being signs of God's love.

We have each been given a stone and, during the evening, we are going to build a cairn. This cairn will celebrate our meeting as God's living stones on this holy ground – part of our journey together in God's company.

Song	**Will you come and follow me?** (*Common Praise*) OR **Do not be afraid** (*Hymns Old and New: One church, one faith, one Lord*)
Reading	Adapted from **Isaiah 43** Do not fear, for I have redeemed you; I have called you by name; you are mine. When you pass through the waters, I will be with you; and through the rivers, they shall not overwhelm you; when you walk through fire you shall not be burned, and the flame shall not consume you. For I am the Lord your God, the Holy One of Israel, your Saviour. You are precious in my sight, and honoured, and I love you. Do not fear, for I am with you.
Responses	The day draws to a close and night approaches **But we will not be afraid.** God meets us here on this holy ground **We welcome God.** God knows each one of us by name **We rejoice and give thanks.** We are invited to follow God's way **We will put our trust in God.**

God asks us to be living stones
We will build God's kingdom here on earth.

Song	**Oh, where are you going?** (*Heaven Shall Not Wait*) OR **One more step along the world I go** (*Common Praise*)
Reading	**1 Peter 2.4–10**
Music	**Let nothing trouble you** (Bernadette Farrell)
Silence	*There is a short time of silence*
Cairn Building	*We are invited to place our stones on the cairn*
Song	**I will be with you** (*Be Still and Know*) OR **God's Spirit is in my heart** (*Laudate*)
Prayers	Lord, we have stopped for a while in your presence as companions on the way. We pray that you will stay with us as we leave this place and journey on. **Lord, hear our prayer.**
	Lord, we pray that, as your living stones, we may be signs of your kingdom and bearers of your love to all whom we meet. **Lord, hear our prayer.**
	Lord, when times are difficult and we cannot see the way ahead help us to follow you. **Lord, hear our prayer.**

Lord, when our faith falters and we feel empty inside may we meet fellow travellers to sustain us.
Lord, hear our prayer.

Lord, give us the strength and the courage to be signs for those who have lost their way.
Lord, hear our prayer.

Lord, we give thanks for signs of the saints who have gone before. May we follow in their footsteps.
Lord, hear our prayer.

Song
We are marching
(*Hymns Old and New: One church, one faith, one Lord*)
OR
Teach me to dance
(*Hymns Old and New: One church, one faith, one Lord*)

Blessing
May God's blessing be on each one of us
May God's blessing be on our journeys
May God's blessing keep us in safety and in peace.
Amen

LENT

In this service, after the silence, everyone is invited to come and take away one of the stones which have been put on the ground spelling 'Father, forgive'. These stones are to be taken away and carried around as reminders, during Lent, of the many times we fall short of building God's kingdom here on earth, now. At the end of Lent everyone is invited to decorate their stones with bright coloured patterns or words and bring them back to church on Easter Day. The stones will then be arranged on the floor to spell 'Alleluia'. The stones, which have been representing our sins, will have been transformed, as our sins are by Jesus dying on the cross for us – from a burden to a colourful 'Alleluia'.

You will need
- A collection of fairly large pebbles, laid out on the floor to spell 'Father forgive'
- CD player
- CD of *Gift of God* by Marty Haugen
- A cross
- Candles

Preparation
Arrange the chairs in a semi-circle around the 'Father, forgive' stones.
The stones can be on the floor at the foot of the cross
Light the candles and place around the stones.

Whichever one of you has committed no sin may throw the first stone at her.
John 8.7

Welcome
Tonight we have come together to spend some time reflecting on the meaning of Lent. In Lent we are given the opportunity

to stop and look at ourselves, to see if there are areas in our lives which we might want to change. This might involve stopping something or starting something, it might involve changing life-patterns. Lent is a time to heighten our awareness of God in our everyday living. It is a time to stop, to look and to listen to God.

Song

God forgave my sin
(*Hymns Old and New: New Anglican Edition*)
OR
I, the Lord of sea and sky
(*Common Praise*)

Psalm

Psalm 51.1–10
Say alternate verses

Reading

John 8.1–11

Reflection

The woman in the story has been caught committing adultery. What might we be caught doing if all our wrongs were exposed?
Father, forgive us.

In the story others accuse the woman. How often have we accused others with malice and delight?
Father, forgive us.

In the story people take delight in someone else's wrongs. How often have we gossiped about what we think others have done, and enjoyed the tittle tattle?
Father, forgive us.

In the story Jesus forgives the woman and says, 'Go, but do not sin again.' How many times has Jesus forgiven us, and yet we have done the same thing again?
Father, forgive us.

In the story we are reminded again of God's wonderful patience and love for us. God's forgiveness is always there for us whenever we say 'sorry'.
Thanks be to God.

Music   **Kyrie** (Marty Haugen)

Silence   *We will now spend some time in silence thinking about the many things we have done that burden us and for which we would like to be forgiven. Those wrongs we have done to others, those wrongs we have done to ourselves. They will be many and varied, but because of them none of us are able to throw the first stone. At the end of the silence we are invited to come and pick up a stone from those on the ground that spell 'Father, forgive'. We may keep the stone as a reminder during Lent that we cannot throw the first stone. We may choose to carry the stone in our pocket. At the end of Lent we may decorate the stone, in bright resurrection colours, and come to church on Easter Sunday to lay it down with others to spell a new word – 'Alleluia'. The stones will have been transformed. Each one of us has the opportunity to be forgiven and transformed on Easter Day, and every time we say 'sorry'*

Song   **From heaven you came**
                   (*Common Praise*)
                   OR
                   Lord, we turn to you for mercy
                   (*Hymns Old and New: One church, one faith, one Lord*)

The Lord's Prayer

Song   **Keep watch with me**
                   (*Be Still and Know*)
                   OR
                   Give thanks with a grateful heart
                   (*Hymns Old and New: New Anglican Edition*)

Blessing

As we journey through Lent carrying our stones, we ask God's help and blessing.

Amen

As we reflect upon the things we have done wrong and try to change them, we ask God's blessing.

Amen

As we look to Easter with hopes and expectations of the freedom of forgiveness that it will bring, we praise God.

Amen

The blessing of God, Father, Son and Holy Spirit be upon us all as we continue on our journey through Lent.

Amen

MEETING JESUS
UNEXPECTEDLY

You will need
- CD player
- CD of *Feast of Life* by Marty Haugen
- A low table
- A loaf of bread in a basket
- Candles
- Song sheets for everyone
- Five prayer sheets with all ten prayer petitions

Preparation
If possible place chairs in a circle around a central low table.
Place the basket of bread and the candles on the table.
Ask five people to read the prayers – two each.
Have just enough light for people to be able to read.

When he was at table with them, he took bread, gave thanks,
broke it and began to give it to them.
Then their eyes were opened and they recognized him.

Luke 24.30–31

Welcome
Welcome. The theme for this evening has to do with meeting Jesus in unexpected places and at unexpected times. We shall use the story of the Road to Emmaus from Luke's Gospel. Cleopas and another disciple were walking and talking with a stranger three days after Jesus' crucifixion. They reached Emmaus and urged the stranger to stay with them. It was not until he blessed and broke the bread at supper that they recognized Jesus. Then he disappeared from their sight.
We 'meet' Jesus many times and in many places. But how often do we recognize him – even fleetingly?

Song	Sing of one who walks beside us
	(*Laudate*)
	OR
	There is one among us
	(*There Is One Among Us*)

Reading	Luke 24.13–32

Song	Stay with us
	(*Songs from Taizé*)
	OR
	Let us stay together for a time
	(*Iona Abbey Music Book*)

The loaf of bread is held up for all to see
We ask for the Lord's blessing on this loaf of bread which we break to share together in fellowship.
The loaf of bread is broken

Prayers	Risen Lord, we meet you unexpectedly in the breaking of bread.
	Make us aware of your presence.

Risen Lord, we meet you unexpectedly in the stranger at the door.
Make us aware of your presence.

Risen Lord, we meet you unexpectedly in the innocence of a child.
Make us aware of your presence.

Risen Lord, we meet you unexpectedly in words of forgiveness.
Make us aware of your presence.

Risen Lord, we meet you unexpectedly in the kindness of our neighbour.
Make us aware of your presence.

Risen Lord, we meet you unexpectedly in the face of the frightened.
Make us aware of your presence.

Risen Lord, we meet you unexpectedly at the bedside of the dying.
Make us aware of your presence.

Risen Lord, we meet you unexpectedly in the addict on the street.
Make us aware of your presence.

Risen Lord, we meet you unexpectedly in the prisoner whom we visit.
Make us aware of your presence.

Risen Lord, we meet you unexpectedly in the silence of our hearts.
Make us aware of your presence.

Silence   *There is now a time of silence lasting about 10 minutes*

Action   *The loaf of bread is passed around and shared*

Music   **On the Journey to Emmaus** (Marty Haugen)

Prayer   Risen Lord, we thank you for the bread and the fellowship we have shared this evening. As we go from this place out into the world, may we be more aware of the people around us, knowing that it is in our daily lives that we may meet you, in unexpected places and at the most unexpected times.

Song   **Thanks for the fellowship**
(*Hymns Old and New: One church, one faith, one Lord*)
OR
May you walk with Christ beside you
(*Laudate*)

MENTAL HEALTH

Websites   www.mind.org.uk, www.sane.org.uk, www.mdf.org.uk
               www.samaritans.org.uk, www.alzheimers.org.uk
               www.youngminds.org.uk, www.rethink.org
               www.mentalhealth.org.uk

You will need
- CD player
- CDs of gentle music including *Fire of Love* by Margaret Rizza
- Flowers and candles
- Incense sticks or fragrant oil to burn
- If you have an indoor water pump you can include a water feature with stones
- Service sheets for everyone

Preparation   If you have chairs place them loosely in the round.
               Cushions and rugs will make the space more inviting.
               In the middle of the circle create a beautiful focus with
               flowers, candles, incense or oil.
               Gentle music plays as everyone arrives.

Peace I leave with you; my peace I give to you.

John 14.27

Welcome   Today we focus on mental health, a subject that affects most of
                us at some time during our lives. We find it so much easier to
                deal with illness that is visible. When we are faced with a men-
                tal illness that is not so visible – either our own, or a member
                of our family, or someone we know – it is hard to know what
                to do or what to say. But God names us and knows us just as

we are. So this evening we are going to listen to some short readings and sing some quiet songs. We shall have a time of stillness and a time to share God's peace with one another.

Song	**Christ's is the world (A touching place)** (*Hymns Old and New: One church, one faith, one Lord*) OR **Healer of our every ill** (*Laudate*)
Reading	Isaiah 43.1–7
Song/Reading	**O God, you search me (Psalm 139)** (*Laudate*) OR **Psalm 139**
Reading	John 14.1 and 27
Song	**We cannot measure** (*Common Praise*) OR **God, you meet us in our weakness** (*Complete Anglican Hymns Old and New*)
Reading	Alternative Beatitudes (Anon)

Blessed are you who do not shun me
but embrace me as I struggle to find the gift within the pain.
Blessed are you who do not shrink from sharing
that you too have known the searing cloud.
Blessed are you who listen
and by listening affirm me as I am.
Blessed are you to tell me I am precious
and worthy of the deepest cherishing.
Blessed are you who fan the tiny flame
that shines more brightly in the dark.
Blessed are you who know me as I am.

Prayer Response	**Lord Jesus Christ, lover of all** (*Laudate*) OR **Jesus Christ, Son of God** (*Heaven Shall Not Wait*)
Prayers	For all those who are troubled or anxious this night that they may find comfort. *Sung response* For psychiatrists, psychologists, community psychiatric nurses, community support workers, social workers, occupational therapists, and all who work in community mental health teams. *Sung response* For those who work in resource centres in our cities and towns, that there may be sufficient financial support. *Sung response* For those whose way of life may be different from ours, that we may have patience and understanding. *Sung response* For ourselves, our families and friends, that we may love and care for one another in times of need. *Sung response*
Music	**Calm me, Lord** (Margaret Rizza)
Stillness	*We sit in stillness for up to 5 minutes*
Song	**Put peace into each other's hands** (*Sing Glory*) OR **Take my hands, Lord** (*Hymns Old and New: One church, one faith, one Lord*)

The Peace	Let us turn to the people next to us to offer a sign of God's peace saying, 'The peace of the Lord be with you'.
Song	**Brother, sister, let me serve you** (*Laudate*) OR **Peace before us** (*Hymns Old and New: One church, one faith, one Lord*)
Blessing	**God's blessing and peace rest on you and me** **God's blessing and peace rest on our families and loved ones** **God's blessing and peace rest on all who are troubled in mind or spirit, this night and in the days to come.** **Amen**

MIDSUMMER

Here is a liturgy for midsummer. Take advantage of the long daylight hours by planning an evening liturgy outdoors. You can either use part of the church-yard or a church hall garden, or even a private garden – whatever seems to lend itself to the occasion.

You will need
- Chairs, stools, rugs and cushions
- CD player
- CD of *Gloria – The sacred music of John Rutter*
- Candles in lanterns or jars so that they stay alight
- Flowers and greenery
- It is suggested that the reading from Genesis is read from *The Message* by Eugene H. Peterson
- Service sheets for everyone

Preparation
Create a worship space on the lawn using the flowers, green-ery and lit candles as a central focus.
Arrange the chairs, stools, rugs and cushions in a circle.

> Earth produced green seed-bearing plants, all varieties,
> and fruit-bearing trees of all sorts.
>
> Genesis 1.12

Welcome
We meet this midsummer evening to celebrate the fullness of God's creation. The earth has turned from the harvest of autumn through the deep sleep of winter. Following winter the first stirrings of new birth in spring now culminate in the abundance and colour of midsummer. We meet outdoors,

under the evening sky, soon to be patterned with stars – at one
with nature.

Opening Response	As a mother raises her child to adulthood **So God brings creation to maturity.**

Let us thank God for the beauty of the earth
We praise and bless you, Creator God.

We are part of this creation, growing to fullness in God,
Thanks be to God.

Song	**Lord of all worlds** (*New Start Hymns and Songs*) OR **Lord, you created** (*Hymns Old and New: One church, one faith, one Lord*)

Reading	Genesis 1–2.4

Song	**In the darkness of the still night** (*Be Still and Know*) OR **For the fruits of all creation** (*Laudate*)

Action	We are now going to join hands as we listen to the following piece of music and keep a short time of silence – as God's continuous cycle of creation reaches the height and fullness of summer let us, too, form a continuous circle that has no beginning and no end.

Recorded Music	**For the beauty of the earth** (John Rutter)

Silence	*There now follows a short period of silence*

Prayer	We thank you, God, for the changing seasons and for the beauty of your earth. We are sorry for the times we have

treated it carelessly, and we pray that we may find ways to restore that which we have spoiled.
Creator God, hear our prayer.

We thank you, God, for the beauty of the skies. We pray that it may not be too late to reverse the damage caused to the ozone layer that protects and shields us.
Creator God, hear our prayer.

We thank you, God, for the sea, sometimes so calm, sometimes so strong and wild, full of wonderful creatures. We pray that we may learn to respect the sea and stop polluting it with things we require no longer.
Creator God, hear our prayer.

We thank you, God, for the joy of human love. We pray that we may bestow on each other that same love that you have so freely given us.
Creator God, hear our prayer.

Song	**Teach me to dance** (*Hymns Old and New: One church, one faith, one Lord*) OR **My Jesus, my Saviour** (*Sing Glory*)
Closing Responses	As evening draws in and darkness falls **So we too prepare to take our rest.** We have spent time with God and with each other **We have sung God's song and rejoiced in God's beauty.** The day is almost ended and we shall depart in peace **Thanks be to God.**
Blessing	**May God, the artist of creation, who paints nature in rainbow colours, and humanity in rich diversity, keep us in safety and bless us.** Amen

We sing the following song as we slowly depart and go our separate ways

Leaving Song **The peace of the earth be with you**
(*Hymns Old and New: One church, one faith, one Lord*)
OR
Glory and gratitude and praise
(*Iona Abbey Music Book*)

NATIONAL OR
INTERNATIONAL TRAGEDY

You will need
- CD player
- CD of *Gift of God* by Marty Haugen
- A focal point which in some way illustrates the tragedy – possibly the name of the place or people involved
- Photographs from the press
- A sign saying 'Father, forgive'
- A selection of lit candles of various sizes
- A basket containing unlit nightlights
- If suitable a pen with a card for people to sign, to send to those involved in the tragedy
- A low table
- Service sheets for everyone

Preparation

If possible place the chairs in a circle around the focal point.
Place the signs or pictures among the lit candles.
Place the basket of nightlights and the pen and card on a low table.

He will wipe away all tears from their eyes. There will be no more death, no more grief or crying or pain.

Revelation 21.4

Welcome

Welcome. We have come together tonight to share our pain and bewilderment about what has happened in . . . Our emotions are tossed around as we try to make some sense of everything. So we gather here as God's frightened, sad children and know that God is with us and holding us.

Song	**Be still my soul** (*Hymns Old and New: New Anglican Edition*) OR **Be still and know that I am God** (*Hymns Old and New: New Anglican Edition*)
Psalm	**Psalm 17.6–13** *Read alternate verses*
Reading	**Revelation 21.1–7**
Music	**Neither Death nor Life** (Marty Haugen)
Silence	*There is now a time of silence lasting about 10 minutes*
Action and Song	**O Christe Domine Jesu** (O Christ, Lord Jesus) (*Songs and Prayers from Taizé*) *As we start singing the song anyone who wants to is invited to light a candle as a sign of hope that God's light will warm and heal the hearts and minds of those who grieve. If there is a card it can be signed by those who go to light a candle* *The song will be sung a few times and then the prayers will be said with* **O Christe Domine Jesu** *sung as the response between each prayer*
Prayer	God our Father, God our Mother; we come before you as bewildered children, unable to understand the enormity of this tragedy which has profoundly touched us yet has not directly affected us. Our heads know that you would never will such a tragedy. Our hearts cry out, 'Why? Why, O Lord? Why?' Comfort us tonight, O God, hold us close to you and share our grief. *Sung response* Our Lord Jesus Christ wept when his friend Lazarus died; he knew the pain and sadness of a human life, of human suffering, of human death. We pray for all those who have died (*whether victims or perpetrators – all are victims in one way or another*). Let your love enfold them and grant them rest eternal. *Sung response*

Holy Spirit of God, sustainer and comforter, grant your loving presence to the bereaved, to parents, brothers and sisters, families and the greater community. All affected in their own way. Be with them as they grieve and help them to exorcise the horror and fear that they may be feeling. We pray that they may come to find a place of peace.
Sung response

Holy and blessed Trinity, Creator, Redeemer and Sustainer, be with us all as we share the pain of our fellow human beings. Comfort us with your love and bring us to a realization of your peace, which passes all understanding.
Sung response

Continue singing until **Amen** *is sung*

Blessing

God will wipe away all the tears from their eyes
Your kingdom come. Your will be done.
There will be no more death
Your kingdom come. Your will be done.
There will be no more grief
Your kingdom come. Your will be done.
There will be no more crying
Your kingdom come. Your will be done.
There will be no more pain
Your kingdom come. Your will be done.
God's blessing be upon all who grieve,
all who walk with them,
and all who are gathered here tonight to pray for them.
Amen
Let us go out into the world in peace and love.
Amen

PEACE

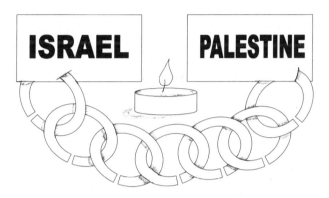

You will need
- A large cross
- Pairs of cards to go at the foot of the cross – write the names of two countries on each pair, or two opposing situations that need healing – make several pairs as shown in the illustration at the back of the book, page 179
- Cut out 'hope love peace' chain links – at least one for each person using the template at the back of the book, page 180
- Cut out lots of plain chain links, make chains, and attach to the pairs of cards
- Quiet music
- CD of *Go Before Us* by Bernadette Farrell
- CD player
- Service sheets – each one containing one loose 'love, hope, peace' link
- Nightlights
- Low tables

Preparation	If possible set the chairs in a semi-circle around the focal point.
	Put the cross at the centre of the display and place the cards and chains around the foot of the cross. Some of the cards can be placed on low tables at different heights and some can go on the floor.
	Place lit nightlights among the cards.

. . . he broke down the wall that separated them and kept them enemies.

Ephesians 2.14b

Welcome	Tonight we have come together to focus on and pray for those parts of our lives, and the places in the world, that are not at peace with each other. We are going to break the chains that cause situations to be trapped and held in a cycle of disharmony and hatred – those places and situations where the history of the past prevents any hope of change coming about in the future. We are going to focus on them and pray for peace and love to come to them. We know that situations that seem impossible to change can be changed – apartheid in South Africa and the Berlin Wall being obvious examples. For we must remember and believe that with God nothing is impossible.
Song	**My peace** (*Be Still and Know*) OR **Peace, perfect peace, is the gift** (*Hymns Old and New: New Anglican Edition*)
Psalm	**Psalm 5** *Say alternate verses*
Reading	**Ephesians 2.12–22** *Everyone turns to face the reader*
Intercessions	In our hearts and in our minds let us break the chains of hatred and distrust that stifle and hold us down and won't allow us to

reach out to our brothers and sisters. Let us find a new way of peace and harmony in our lives.
Listen to my voice, O Lord
And hear my sighs.
Listen to my cry for help
My God and King!

In our hearts and in our minds let us reach out to all those communities who are unable to break the chains of small-mindedness and gossip. Where fear of change and fear of the stranger stop any chance of new ways and new growth from happening.
Listen to my voice, O Lord
And hear my sighs.
Listen to my cry for help
My God and King!

In our hearts and in our minds let us reach out to all people in authority – those who are ensnared by the burden of bureau-cracy chaining them to ever-increasing rules and regulations, and who are unaware of the effect their actions have on others; those who want change but dare not show it for fear of the ridicule it will provoke; and situations where the Spirit cannot fly free and creative thoughts and ideas are squashed.
Listen to my voice, O Lord
And hear my sighs.
Listen to my cry for help
My God and King!

In our hearts and in our minds let us reach out to all places in the world where the history of the past burdens and chains people and stops them finding peace in the future. Where the stories of the past are passed down from generation to genera-tion, and the hatred that goes with them gets handed on and on. We hold out to God those who dare to try to make a dif-ference, those who risk their lives to make things change and those who are chain-breakers, who believe that miracles can and do happen.

Listen to my voice, O Lord
And hear my sighs.
Listen to my cry for help
My God and King!

So let us tonight pray that we might be chain-breakers, peace-makers, hope-carriers, light-bringers. Let us believe in miracles. Let us believe that even we, so unimportant in the scale of things, can and should strive to make a difference, here in our families, our communities, our country and our precious and fragile world.
Listen to my voice, O Lord
And hear my sighs.
Listen to my cry for help
My God and King!

The Lord's Prayer

Music	**Peace Child** (Bernadette Farrell)
Action	*There is now a time of silence lasting about 10 minutes. At the foot of the cross are pairs of different situations in which there is division. These divisions can be between people or countries, or where there are local disputes – where people or situations seem unable to live together in peace and harmony. Between each pair is a chain made from paper links. These links represent the burden of each situation, weighing it down and stopping it from being able to move forward to find peace, healing and love. We are invited to take the chain links in our service sheets, break the chains holding the two situations together, and rejoin them with our links of love, hope and peace*
Song	**Make me a channel of your peace** (*Hymns Old and New: One church, one faith, one Lord*) OR **Come and fill (Confitemini Domino)** (*Songs and Prayers from Taizé*)

Blessing

May the Love of God allow us to turn and love the other
May the inspiration and example of Christ allow us to risk
being chain-breakers
May the Spirit make us fly over barriers to places unknown
and adventures unimaginable
May we trust in God, Father, Son and Holy Spirit.
Amen

PENTECOST

You will need
- CD player
- CD of *Go Before Us* by Bernadette Farrell
- Some unlit nightlights
- Some small paper boats. See the paper boat illustration and follow the instructions at the back of the book, page 181
- A large bowl of water
- A selection of different types of whistles
- Service sheets for everyone
- Some lit candles of different sizes
- A sign saying, 'Come, Holy Spirit'
- A low table

Preparation

If possible arrange the chairs in a circle.

Have some rugs or cushions in case people want to sit on the floor.

Create a focal point on the low table using the candles and the sign.

Arrange the unlit candles, the paper boats and the bowl of water, and the whistles, in such a way that people can get to them after the silence.

They were all filled with the Holy Spirit.

Acts 2.4

Welcome

Welcome. We are gathered here tonight to reflect on the story of Pentecost. The coming of the Holy Spirit. When the disciples were filled with God's Holy Spirit at Pentecost, they discovered they were able to go and do things they never dreamt they were capable of. How wonderful and how frightening! How often do we say, 'Oh, I can't possibly do that'? Well, God often says to us, 'Yes, you can', and God also says, 'I won't expect you to do it alone. I am here with you.' With God's Spirit within us, everything is possible.

In a while we will have a time of silence, so we can reflect on where or when the Holy Spirit comes into our lives. Are we responding to the nudging we get from God, or are we saying, 'No, no, not me'? We are given so many gifts which are there waiting to be used. But often, though we have it within us to use these gifts, we choose not to. Are we like a whistle which, without someone blowing into it, makes no noise? Or are we like a paper boat which cannot float free if it isn't put onto the water? Or are we like a candle which is just a boring old candle if no one sets it alight? If you feel like it, after the silence, go and light a candle to show you want the Holy Spirit to set you alight. Float a paper boat on the water to show you want to free yourself from the things that hold you back. Or blow a whistle to show you want to make a noise for God, and shout about the Good News to everyone you meet.

Song	**Take this moment** (*Hymns Old and New: One church, one faith, one Lord*)) OR **God's Spirit is in my heart** (*Hymns Old and New: New Anglican Edition*)
Reading	**Acts 2.1–12**
Silence	*There is now a time of silence lasting about 10 minutes*
Music	**If today you hear God's voice** (Bernadette Farrell)
Action	*If you feel like it, while the music is playing, go and light a candle, float a boat or blow a whistle*
Prayer	Come Holy Spirit **Fill us with excitement.**

Come Holy Spirit
Fill us with amazement.
Come Holy Spirit
Fill us with your wonder.
Come Holy Spirit
Free our tongues to proclaim God's love.
Come Holy Spirit
Free our tongues to find the right words.
Come Holy Spirit
Free our tongues to break down barriers.
Come Holy Spirit
Be a strong wind and open our hearts to welcome God's love.
Come Holy Spirit
Light us up with your fire to shine as God's light in the world.
Come Holy Spirit
Come Holy Spirit.

Song   **Veni Sancte Spiritus** (Come Holy Spirit)
                  (*Songs from Taizé*)
                  OR
                  Spirit of the living God (Iverson)
                  (*Hymns Old and New – New Anglican Edition*)

Blessing   Let us be like a rushing wind blowing away the hatred and hurt
                  in God's world.
                  Amen
                  Let us breathe the breath of God's peace on all whom we meet.
                  Amen
                  Let us be the fire in God's world which brings light to the dark-
                  est places.
                  Amen
                  May the blessing of God's Holy Spirit be upon us tonight and
                  always.
                  Amen and Amen
                  Let us go and be full of wonder, excitement and amazement
                  In the name of Christ.
                  Amen

PRISONERS

Websites   www.prisonersfamilies.org.uk
www.prisonersabroad.org.uk
www.amnesty.org

You will need
- Two lengths of chain either made of paper or light metal
- One large candle on a stand
- Candles – different sizes
- A basket of nightlights
- Names of local or national prisons on cards
- Known international situations where prisoners are being held
- Cards with bent prison bars – enough for everyone. See the prison bars template at the back of the book, page 182
- CD player
- CD of *River of Peace* by Margaret Rizza
- CD of *The Sound of Kings* (Vaughan Williams)
- A low table – you may need two
- Service sheets for everyone or words on an OHP

Preparation   Create a display on the table(s) with the candles – wind the
                   two lengths of chain between them and down each side.
                   Light the candles but leave the large candle unlit.
                   Place the basket of nightlights and cards within easy reach.

At once all the prison doors flew open, and everybody's chains came loose.

                                                                    Acts 16.26

Welcome   This evening we gather to worship together and to think about
                   prisoners.

                   Being a 'prisoner' can mean many different things. We think of
                   prisoners generally as people who have done wrong and who
                   are paying the price for their wrongdoing by being locked
                   away from society for a set period of time. In some countries
                   people are imprisoned as a 'punishment' for having opinions
                   and views which challenge the state. They dare to speak out
                   knowing the risk they take. Amnesty International is an organ-
                   ization that works hard on behalf of 'prisoners of conscience'.
                   And there are those who are kidnapped by terrorists for polit-
                   ical reasons – their imprisonment is a terrible ordeal for both
                   them and their families.

                   Many of us are prisoners, through ill health or fear or addic-
                   tion. We may be unable to leave our homes because of illness
                   or disability – or agoraphobia. And sometimes we create our
                   own prisons which keep us trapped inside ourselves and pre-
                   vent us from living in freedom. People around us may be quite
                   unaware of the 'prisons' we experience.

Song   **God's Spirit is in my heart**
                   (*Hymns Old and New: New Anglican Edition*)
                   OR
                   We are young, we are old (Jubilee Song)
                   (*Restless Is the Heart*)

Opening   Jesus, you came to bring good news to the poor
Responses   **We hold up to you those imprisoned by poverty.**

Jesus, you came to bind up the broken-hearted
We hold up to you those imprisoned by sorrow.

Jesus, you came to set the captives free
We hold up to you all those in prison.

Jesus, you came to proclaim the year of the Lord's favour
We hold up to you all those imprisoned by debt.

Jesus, you came to comfort all who mourn,
We hold up to you those imprisoned by grief.

Song	**O God, you search me** (*Hymns Old and New: One church, one faith, one Lord*) OR **Shepherd me, O God** (*Laudate*)
Reading	**Acts 16.22–34** *After this reading the chains are 'broken' in two and separated and the large candle is lit*
Reading	**A Reading from Viktoras Petkus, Lithuania** You come through thick stone walls, armed guards and bars: you bring me a starry night and ask me about this and that. You are the Redeemer. I recognize you. You are my way, my truth and my life. Even my cellar blooms with stars and peace and light pours forth. You sprinkle beautiful words on me like flowers: 'Son, what are you afraid of? I am with you!'
Song	**God to enfold you** (*Hymns Old and New: One church, one faith, one Lord*) OR **Christ be beside me** (*Celebration Hymnal for Everyone*)
Music	**Come, my way** (Margaret Rizza) OR **The Call** (from 'Five Mystical Songs' by Vaughan Williams)

Action   *While we listen to the music we are now invited to come forward to light a candle for someone we know who needs the light and peace of God's freedom in their life. We may also take a card to keep*

Prayer   *After each prayer petition we sing*
My eyes are dim with weeping
(There Is One Among Us)
OR
Don't be afraid
(Come All You People)

Holy God, you sent your Son Jesus to bring good news to the poor. We pray for all those who are imprisoned by poverty. We pray for a fairer world where the riches you graciously provide may be shared more equally among your people.
Lord, hear our prayer and lead us to freedom.
Sung response

Holy God, you sent your Son Jesus to bind up the broken-hearted. We pray that we may care for one another with compassion.
Lord, hear our prayer and lead us to freedom.
Sung response

Holy God, you sent your Son Jesus to set the captives free. We pray for prisoners and their families that they might know your redeeming love in the midst of their troubles. We pray, too, for all people whose fear, addiction or illness causes them to create invisible prisons.
Lord, hear our prayer and lead us to freedom.
Sung response

Holy God, you sent your Son Jesus to proclaim the year of the Lord's favour. We pray for agencies campaigning to 'drop the debt' owed by the poorest countries to the richest.
Lord, hear our prayer and lead us to freedom.
Sung response

Holy God, you sent your Son Jesus to comfort all who mourn.
We pray for all those grieving at this time. May they come to
know your presence with them in their pain and loss.
Lord, hear our prayer and lead us to freedom.
Sung response

The Lord's Prayer

Song	**And can it be**
	(*Common Praise*)
	OR
	The Spirit lives to set us free (Walk in the Light)
	(*Hymns Old and New: New Anglican Edition*)
Blessing	**May the love of God break down barriers**
	May the light of God shine in the darkness
	May the peace of God fill us with hope
	May the freedom of God release us
	May the blessing of God rest upon us.
	Amen

REFUGEES AND ASYLUM
SEEKERS

You will need
- CD player
- CD of the musical *Godspell* – based on the Gospel of Matthew
- One large lit candle
- Unlit candles and drip shields for everyone
- Four people, apart from the leader, to be Voices One, Two, Three and Four
- Either a PowerPoint slide show continuously showing silent images of civil war or ethnic violence, or a display of pictures from newspapers and magazines showing the same

Preparation
Place the lit candle at the front and ask the speakers to stand on each side.
The PowerPoint presentation can be shown on a screen above them – or the display can be on boards on each side.
Give everyone an unlit candle and drip shield.
The words to the songs and the psalm should be available – either on the screen or on sheets.

How can we sing the songs of the Lord while in a foreign land?
Psalm 137.4

Welcome
Welcome to our Evening Prayer. This evening we are thinking about refugees and asylum seekers – all those who have come to this land seeking a place of safety and acceptance. In a moment we are going to read Psalm 137 together. The

psalmist asks, 'How can we sing the songs of the Lord while in a foreign land?' We are going to turn this around and reflect on what it might mean to us, here, to be in a 'foreign land'. We will attempt to stand in the shoes of people who have had to leave home and all that is familiar.

Song

Alleluia! Raise the gospel
(*Go Before Us*)
OR
When God almighty came to earth
(*Complete Anglican Hymns Old and New*)

Psalm 137

Read this together out loud

Voice One

We were in danger. Everyday life was becoming intolerable. Our homes were in the middle of a civil war zone. We were being abused, physically and mentally, because we were ethnically different from others around us.

We had to leave – and in a hurry. No time to pack cases or say goodbye. The moment came when we had the opportunity to escape – with little more than what we stood up in – and we seized it.

The journey was terrifying. We were in a truck. It was dark. We were hungry and very, very thirsty. There was little air. We were not sure where we were being taken. We were not sure we would survive.

After what seemed like an endless journey we found ourselves here in this place. Where were we? People were speaking to us. But what were they saying? We did not understand. Their faces were not welcoming.

Voice Two

Now, some time later, we are sheltered with others in old army barracks. Some people have been very kind to us and given us the bare essentials for living. We have warm clothes and money to buy food and we have access to doctors. Others have been hostile demanding, 'What are you doing here in our country, taking our resources when there is little enough for our own people?'

Song	**O God, we bear the imprint of your face** (*Sing Glory*) OR **Nada te turbe (Nothing can trouble)** (*Songs from Taizé*)
Voice Three	We would say to you, 'Listen to our pain. Try to understand what we have left behind. We know we are strangers in a foreign land. We would not be here, like this, if we had not been desperate. What would you have done? All these things are new and different for us – language, routine, money, food, school, local customs, weather. We have left behind family and loved ones, friends, our employment, our hobbies, our social status, our animals, the things that give us our identity. We grieve for so much that we have lost.'
Music	**On the willows** (from *Godspell*)
Silence	*There is a short period of silence. If we were stripped of all that is familiar and placed in a foreign land what would we miss most of all?*
Song	**There is a longing** (*Laudate*) OR **Let there be love** (*Hymns Old and New: One church, one faith, one Lord*)
Voice Four	It could work, you know. We bring gifts and abilities that we can offer for the good of all. We want to earn our living. We can learn from each other. Be patient with us as we slowly adapt some of our ways so that they sit more comfortably with yours. Help us to 'sing the songs of the Lord in this strange land'. We are one family in God – brothers and sisters. Let us rejoice in our diversity and learn to live together in love and unity.

Song	**Longing for light (Christ, be our light)**
	(*Laudate*)
	OR
	Brother, sister, let me serve you
	(*Common Praise*)

Throughout history people have fled to avoid persecution. We are now going to hear two short readings from Matthew's Gospel when Mary, Joseph and Jesus have to flee 'to another place' of safety to escape danger.

Reading	**Matthew 2.13–15 and Matthew 2.19–23**
Action	We will now light our candles.
	The leader lights a candle and passes the light to the person on each side. The light is passed from person to person until all the candles are lit
Prayers	*Between each of the petitions sing*
	Within our darkest night
	(*Songs from Taizé*)
	OR
	Kindle a flame
	(*Heaven Shall Not Wait*)

That hearts may be warmed by the fire of your love and that those who seek refuge and safety may be made welcome
Lord, we pray.
Sung response

That what is unknown and fearful may become familiar and safe and that suspicion and prejudice may be replaced with trust and acceptance
Lord, we pray.
Sung response

That grief and sorrow may be healed by compassion and that generosity of spirit and love for neighbour may be visible in our lives
Lord, we pray.
Sung response

That we may grow in knowledge and understanding and that we may all 'sing the songs of the Lord' together, in harmony
Lord, we pray.
Sung response

The candles are extinguished

Song

When I needed a neighbour
(*Complete Anglican Hymns Old and New*)
OR
We have a dream
(*Hymns Old and New: One church, one faith, one Lord*)

The Peace

May the peace of Christ enfold us
May the love of Christ surround us
May the hope of Christ fill our lives
Let us share a sign of peace and love and hope together.

All greet one another

Let us go from this place in peace
Thanks be to God!

REMEMBRANCE

You will need • A PowerPoint presentation or display of pictures of situations of conflict, either off the Internet or from the press, or the names of places where conflict is happening
 • CD player
 • CD of quiet instrumental music
 • Peace cards. See the 'Let there be peace' template at the back of the book, page 183
 • Candles of different sizes
 • A sand tray and basket of unlit candles
 • A low table

Preparation Create a focus on the table with the pictures, words and lit candles.
Everyone will need a service sheet.

'But now I tell you: love your enemies and pray for those who persecute you.'

Matthew 5.44

Welcome This evening we gather to reflect and remember those who have died in wars. To pray that warring should cease and that a new way of peace and love should be found in all areas of the world. We reflect on Jesus' simple message of Love. We know in our hearts that this is the way forward to finding a lasting peace which will enable God's kingdom to be built here on earth, now. We also know, sadly, that we seem unable or unwilling to embrace this simple message and be kingdom-builders.

Song **Peace, perfect peace, is the gift**
(*Hymns Old and New: New Anglican Edition*)
OR
Let there be love
(*Hymns Old and New: New Anglican Edition*)

Reading **Matthew 5.43–48**

Song **Lord, we come to ask your healing**
(*Hymns Old and New: New Anglican Edition*)
OR
Lead me from death to life (Prayer for Peace)
(*Be Still and Know*)

Prayers O God our Father! O God our Mother! How can we, your fragile children, pray to you and listen to your voice when we are overwhelmed by the discord that surrounds us? Hatred is so noisy, so overwhelming, so all-consuming, so destructive. We pray that we will find a place of peace in our hearts, a place of harmony, a place of listening and stillness.
Lord in your mercy
Bring us peace.

O God our Father! O God our Mother! Having found this internal place of peace, we pray that we will bring that inner

peace to all areas of our lives – into our homes, into our places of work, and into our times of relaxation. We pray we will be bearers of your light, love and peace wherever we go.
That we will continually strive to ask ourselves, 'Is this God's way or my way?'
Lord in your mercy
Bring us peace.

O God our Father! O God our Mother! All over the world there are conflicts. There are groups of people who live on hatred and war – those who know they are right and that others are wrong. There are people who fight for their causes and who kill all those who get in their way. We pray that a new way of respect for the other will be found, a way of talking rather than warring and, through that, a way of healing.
Lord in your mercy
Bring us peace.

O God our Father! O God our Mother! We remember tonight those thousands upon thousands who left their homes and families to fight for freedom for themselves and for others, and in so doing were killed or injured – those who recognized evil when they saw it, those who gave their lives so that others might live in peace. We pray that those lives were not given in vain – that the battles that were won for our freedom should never have to be fought again.
Lord in your mercy
Bring us peace.

O God our Father! O God our Mother! We pray that all countries who deal in weapons, both making them and trading them, may find a way to trade in love and poverty-breaking, rather than hatred and debt-building.
Lord in your mercy
Bring us peace.

Music   *Quiet instrumental music is played to lead into silence*

Silence	*There is now a time of silence lasting about 10 minutes*
Action	*After the silence, if you wish, you are invited to come to the front to light candles in memory of the millions of people who have died as a result of war. The images which the candles surround remind us of how very destructive we can be, and how very dark we can make God's beautiful world. We light candles to dispel that darkness. Please take a card away as a reminder that, if peace can start in our own hearts and minds even in this small way, it will begin to affect others on the national and international stage*
Music	*Quiet instrumental music is played while candles are lit*

Song

Lord Jesus Christ
(*Songs from Taizé*)
OR
Nothing can trouble
(*Songs and Prayers from Taizé*)

Responses

In our hurt and pain
Let us, with your help, God, bring healing.

In our struggle and chaos
Let us, with your help, God, bring calm and serenity.

In our wars and conflicts
Let us, with your help, God, bring peace and understanding.

In our dying and death
Let us, with your help, God, see life renewed and a new beginning.

Song

God is Love: let heaven adore him
(*Hymns Old and New: New Anglican Edition*)
OR
O day of peace
(*Laudate*)

Blessing   May the God of Love dispel hatred
May the God of Peace bring harmony to places in confusion and conflict.
May the God of Light overwhelm dark things happening in dark places
May the God of Hope inspire peacemakers.
May God bless us as we leave here tonight and may we be aware of God's ever-loving presence wherever we go
Let us go in peace to love and serve the Lord.

Let us offer each other a sign of peace

THE LORD'S PRAYER

Websites   www.v-a.com/bible/prayer.html
Website with words and sound of the original Aramaic that
Jesus would have spoken
www.christusrex.org
This website has the Lord's Prayer translated into 1310
different languages
There are many other websites looking at the Lord's Prayer.
Just put 'Lord's Prayer' into the search box on your computer
and enjoy what you find!

You will need
- CD player and any of the following CDs including the Lord's
  Prayer
  CD of *The Lord's Prayer* by Ash Family and Friends (the Lord's
  Prayer is repeated 33 times)
  CD of *Hopes and Dreams – A New Musical for a New
  Millennium*
  CD of *African Sanctus* by David Fanshawe
  CD of *Joy on Earth* from the Taizé Community
  CD of *Celtic Daily Prayer* from the Northumbria Community
  CDs of music for Station 6, eg the 'Hallelujah Chorus' from
  Handel's *Messiah* or 'Sanctus' from Karl Jenkins' *The Armed
  Man: A mass for peace*
- A projector if pictures are to be shown
- A low table for each station display
- Different sized lit candles, unlit nightlights and a tray of sand

Hymns   **Our Father** (Caribbean)
(*Hymns Old and New: One church, one faith, one Lord*)
Our Father (Wiener)
(*Hymns Old and New: One church, one faith, one Lord*)

Father God in Heaven
(*Praise God Together*)
Our Father
(*Laudate*)
Our Father
(*Celebration Hymnal for Everyone*)
Forgive our sins as we forgive
(*Hymns Old and New: New Anglican Edition*)

Preparation	The space should be arranged so that there are six 'stations' around the building, each one depicting a different phrase from the Lord's Prayer.
	In addition to the items indicated separately below, each 'station' will need to have the following:

The particular phrase written out on cards using several different translations and making the words as big as possible so they can be read from a distance.

Different sized candles, nightlights and a tray of sand for people to place their own lighted nightlights.

A small display to 'illustrate' the phrase of the prayer using pictures, objects, or some readings.

Station 1	**Our Father in heaven, Hallowed be your name**
Extra items needed	
	A sheet of paper and pens to write God's names
Layout	The words of the prayer are placed around some candles. Place the large sheet of paper to the side, preferably on a flip chart stand
Action	Invite people to write down different names for God – it is important that each person thinks about what words they use to describe God. Here are some:

- Almighty
- God
- The Supreme Being
- Divine Creator
- Deus
- Omnipotent Being
- Master of the Universe
- The Creator
- All-Powerful
- Invincible
- Divine
- All-Knowing
- Boundless
- Eternal

- Godly
- Everlasting
- God of God
- Light of Light
- Wonderful

- Counsellor
- King of Kings
- Lord of Lords
- Mighty One

Station 2   **Your kingdom come, your will be done, on earth as in heaven**

Extra items needed

A selection of images showing the good and bad things of this world. The good images are arranged under a sign saying, 'God's way' and the bad images under a sign saying, 'Our way'. In and among the images is a list of 'God's way' words: hope, love, joy, peace . . . and among the 'bad' images a list of 'Our way' words: hate, war, fight, kill, jealousy, bitterness . . .

Layout

Place the words from the prayer around some candles. Place the 'good' and 'bad' words and images together on either side of the station.

Station 3   **Give us today our daily bread**

Extra items needed

A small bowl of rice and a large plate of food, eg fish and chips

A large broken communion wafer or loaf of bread

Layout

Place the words by some candles. Arrange the food side by side with the broken communion wafer or loaf of bread lying between the two.

Station 4   **Forgive us our sins as we forgive those who sin against us**

Extra items needed

A very large sign saying, 'Sorry', small pieces of paper, pencils, a cross

Layout

The words of the prayer are placed around the candles. A sign saying 'Sorry' is placed at the foot of the cross. A bowl suitable to burn pieces of paper in is placed at the foot of the cross together with a basket of small pieces of paper and pencils.

| Actions | Invite people to write down the things they want to say sorry for, and then to burn the pieces of paper in the bowl. |

Station 5 — Lead us not into temptation but deliver us from evil

Extra items needed

Temptation words on cards such as 'Self-gratification', 'Who will I hurt?', 'I'll do it despite the consequences', 'Who cares?', 'It won't make any difference', 'I must have it NOW' . . . a selection of ads from magazines describing 'must have' items.

| Layout | The words of the prayer, along with the temptation words and pictures, are placed around the candles. |

Station 6 — For the kingdom, the power, and the glory are yours now and for ever. Amen

Extra items needed

Anything that reflects God's glory – maybe a wonderful arrangement of flowers, or pictures, or beautiful recorded music

| Layout | The words of the prayer are placed around candles and flowers. |
| Action | Play a piece of music that reflects God's glory such as Handel's 'Hallelujah Chorus' from *Messiah* or the 'Sanctus' from Karl Jenkins' *The Armed Man: A mass for peace* |

One of his disciples said to him, 'Lord, teach us to pray'.

Luke 11.1

| Welcome | We are gathered here together to spend time reflecting on the prayer that Jesus taught his disciples when they asked, 'Lord, teach us to pray'. The prayer is broken up into six phrases. Each one is taken in turn and reflected upon. There are many different translations of the prayer and samples of these are placed at each station. It is hoped that this will give a new insight into the meaning of the each section of the prayer. We already have a situation where some churches use the 'new |

words' and some the 'old'. Of course, neither the traditional English nor the newer modern English are the actual words that Jesus spoke.

Option 1 How the evening is planned is very flexible. Each of us can move around from 'station' to 'station' as and when we want. We can spend the whole evening staying with one station, or we can move around the stations in any order. The good thing about this approach is it removes us further from the 'parrot fashion' saying of the prayer.

Option 2 We are going to move around the different stations as a group, much as one would in the more traditional way saying the 'Stations of the cross' used in many churches during Lent. We shall move from one station to the next, singing a different setting of the Lord's Prayer between each station.

We have included three additional alternative resources to use with the Lord's Prayer stations:

The first is a set of reflections to be read at each station, followed by short periods of silence.

The second is a short 'discussion' between a person and God. This could be used at the beginning of the evening, at each station, or at the end of the evening. It might be that people in the congregation would like to write their own conversations with God looking at each part of the prayer – so have paper and pens ready just in case.

The third is a wonderful reflection 'Lord, teach me to pray' which could be used during the evening.

Please use the stations in whatever way seems appropriate – using words, silence, music or action.

Reflections on the Lord's Prayer

Welcome The idea of this evening is to spend time reflecting on the Lord's Prayer. We say this prayer so frequently that often we lose its meaning. There is the risk that we are so familiar with it that we just run through it parrot fashion. This prayer is prayed daily by Christians all over the world. Jesus' disciples asked him in Matthew 6.9–13 and Luke 11.2–4, 'teach us how to pray'. Maybe they had seen Jesus withdraw from them to pray and seen how he changed when he had taken time out to talk and listen to his Father, and they wanted to know how they could also pray and be changed.

Reflection 1
Our Father in heaven

The Lord's Prayer is about our relationship with God and God's relationship with us. On the whole our human fathers and mothers want the best for us. They are concerned for our well-being, our nurture, our nourishment and our health. So, if that is the case with our fathers and mothers on earth, how much greater will our Father in heaven want what is best for us? So, in the first line of the prayer we turn to our heavenly Father, who cares for us in all that we do and say. We turn to be held in God's loving embrace. God is always there waiting for us.

The words in the Lord's Prayer also speak of 'our' Father, not 'my' Father. We are all part of God's community – God's family. God is everyone's Father and Mother. No one has more claim over God than anyone else. God is community, Father, Son and Holy Spirit. We are loved by God and God in turn asks us to love one another, equally. So God is everyone's Father and Mother, your God and my God.

So we, with awareness of God's overwhelming and everlasting presence and love, turn to him when we pray to 'Our Father'.

Hallowed be your name

Although we can call God 'Father', making God very accessible and close to us, we need to recognize that God is also sovereign of the universe, Divine, Eternal, Almighty, way beyond us in our smallness. Yet in that smallness we are allowed to come and draw close to our God. To really live God's way, we need to try to be God's holy people, humble in God's sight, overwhelmed by God's majesty and always recognizing that we want to place God at the centre of our lives. We should want to keep God's name holy, honour God's name at all times and try to live as God's children.

Reflection 2
Your kingdom come
Your will be done
on earth as in heaven

We pray that God's kingdom will come. This implies that it has not come yet. If we are asking that it should come, then we indicate that we have a wish for it to come and be the place where we live. The scary thing about this is that it means we all have to play our part to help make it come, and how we do that is explained in the next line. We do it by God's 'will being done'. God's way of love, God's kingdom, is so often not our way. We only have to pick up a newspaper or watch the news on TV to know that we do not live as God would like us to.

Wars, murder, rape, theft, kidnapping, all scream out at us. We wish that others did not behave in this way. Of course, the reality is that we also behave in this way. A way that is far from God's way. We gossip, we cheat, we lie, we do not love our neighbour. But, of course, we want to think that what 'they' do is much worse than what we do. Often an atrocity occurs 'in the name of humanity'. We all have the capacity to behave in terrible ways – fortunately most of us don't. However because we all fail in big ways, and small, we are culpable for the sin of the world, for failing to make God's kingdom come on earth as in heaven.

Reflection 3
Give us today our daily bread

Here again we are asking not just for ourselves, but for everyone: 'Give us today our daily bread', not 'Give me today my daily bread'. It is in that 'us' and 'our' that God is asking us to share the bountiful gifts we are given. There is the recognition that we all need to be fed, but we are also asked to be aware and responsible for each other.

Of course, the 'daily bread' can be translated to mean much more than food. To survive and flourish as complete human beings, to be living a richness of life, to be God's kingdom-builders, we need to be fed not only with basic food but also spiritual food. The breaking of the bread and the sharing of it is at the heart of what Jesus told us to do, so we need both actual and spiritual food, every day.

The other word we need to be aware of is 'today'. This word reminds us that we need to trust God to give us what we need, at the moment. When the children of Israel were crossing the desert and God gave them the food they needed to survive one day at a time, they found it hard to trust that the manna would come every day. They found, if they gathered more than they needed, it rotted. So we are asking God to feed us with what we need at the present moment, and through this we should trust that it will be enough.

Reflection 4
Forgive us our sins
As we forgive those who sin against us

What a challenge this part of the prayer gives us. Not only are we told that forgiveness is there for us to seek out and take but, having done that, we have to accept that forgiveness. We are then told to do the same by forgiving others. It seems we cannot have the one without the other. Being forgiven, accepting that we are forgiven, and then forgiving others, go together in the prayer. If we want to live God's way, the way of love, we have to take the whole bundle. The forgiveness is there for us to take, unconditionally. If we want to let go of those things we have done and which we regret, we can. By allowing ourselves to be forgiven we are given the chance to start again. As the psalmist puts it 'wash me whiter than snow, put a clean spirit within me'. How wonderful it would be to have nothing hanging around to drag us down. Sometimes it is very hard to accept we are forgiven. To continue to feel bad about something, to let it rumble round and round and to allow it to fill our every moment, seems easier than letting go. This is when we are filled with guilt and anxiety, which in turn can act as a block to allowing God's love to pour into our lives. The challenge of accepting the ending of the guilt can be hard.

Then the prayer goes on to say, having been freed, we should turn round to face those whom we feel have wronged us. As the prayer says, 'as we forgive those who sin against us', or as one translation puts it 'as we forgive the wrongs that others have done to us'.

We cannot accept our freedom without freeing others. But the prayer does *not* say that in order to receive our freedom we *have* to forgive others. There is rather an unconditional understanding that, if we recognize the love God offers us, we will *want* to share it with others and offer them forgiveness and that way we *will* be his kingdom-builders.

Reflection 5
Lead us not into temptation
But deliver us from evil

In this section of the prayer we are again acknowledging our human frailty. We all know that every day we can be led into places of temptation, and that we do not always manage to withstand it. Some of the other translations of this line may help us to see what is being said here. 'Let us not be put to the test', or 'keep us safe from ourselves', help to illustrate what Jesus was saying to us. We are the sinners, but with God's help we can stand against those places of testing. We are given the tools to withstand them if we look at the earlier part of the prayer. If we are to build God's kingdom on earth now, and we are going to do this by following God's way, then we have to put on God's armour of love to protect us from ourselves and each other. If we check out what we are being tempted by and see if it stands up against God's way, we then have the choice to walk away and turn our back on the wrong, or continue to be tempted.

We are very good as humans at finding excuses for doing wrong. We can easily deceive ourselves and be tempted to avoid confronting our sins, but with this prayer we have a way to face the truth about ourselves and confront it.

The next line 'keep us safe from the evil one' or 'deliver us from evil', clearly puts God at the front of the fighting line, offering us God's help to fight, God's protection against all our wrongdoing. Evil often goes on in dark places, because the perpetrator wants it to be hidden. If we shine God's light in those dark places they will be found out. Light will always overcome dark, and as we hold up the light and the love together we will overwhelm the evil.

How do we do this? By continuing our dialogue with God, and by praying as Jesus taught us. Jesus knew so well himself what it was like to be tested, or tempted, in the story in Matthew 4.1–11. Each time the devil tempts Jesus, Jesus holds up God: 'worship the Lord your God and serve only him'. He held up God's way as being the way to overcome the devil. And in Psalm 139.24 we read 'find out if there is any evil in me and guide me in the everlasting way'.

Reflection 6
For the kingdom, the power
and the glory are yours, now and for ever. Amen

It is agreed by most scholars that this final part of the prayer is not part of the Gospel text but was added as part of the prayer at a later date. But it does appear in versions of the prayer as early as the first century, so it is not a modern add-on!

What a wonderful finish. There is nothing better than going out in a blaze of glory. We affirm that God is the ultimate authority, that everything comes from God, and we acknowledge that he is the ruler of his kingdom. He is all-powerful and glorious, and we are prepared to worship him, not ourselves, and to offer our lives as followers of Jesus Christ.

Then we come to the final word, 'Amen'. We say this word so often and yet I wonder how often we think about what it means. Another translation gives us insight: 'Yes, yes, yes!' In other words, 'I agree', 'Here, here!', 'I want to be part of this prayer', 'I want to try to be a kingdom-builder', 'Count me in!'

A Discussion with God

The following dialogue can be spoken by two people. Alternatively give everyone paper and pens and suggest that they write their own conversation with God as they move from station to station.

Our Father in heaven

'Here I am, God. It has been so hard to find time to stop. There was breakfast, then the children to take to school, the house to clear, the washing to hang out. Off to work, the traffic was terrible, got to work late, meetings all day, didn't even have time for lunch. You know how it is.'

'Yes, my child, I know.'

'When I got home it just started again. I know I could have stopped and prayed instead of watching my favourite soap but, God, I was so tired . . .'

'Yes, my child.'

'Now, as I fall asleep, I remember you. I know you told us to pray but, God, I have been so busy. How did the disciples find time to pray, between fishing and rushing around after Jesus?'

'Maybe it was because they saw how stopping and having time to chat with me helped Jesus to check things out, and then return to his busy life. They saw what a difference it made and wanted that difference for themselves. You know that difficult meeting you had today?'

'. . . Yes . . .'

'Well, I could have helped you see a way forward, if you had let me . . . I am your Father. I love you, I am here for you, always, any time of the day or night. Just remember, Jesus taught his disciples to pray because he knew it would change their lives. I want the same for you.'

'Yes, Father.'

Hallowed be your name

'Oh God!'

'Yes, I am here.'

'Jesus, not that again!'

'I am still here.'

'Why are you around? I am not praying at the moment. In fact, rather the opposite. I am really cross. This computer will not do what it is meant to do . . . don't tell me you know how to work a computer as well as everything else?'

'It was you who called me.'

'No, I didn't. You were far from my thoughts. It is the wretched computer that I am thinking about.'

'You said, "Oh God", and "Jesus". Sounded pretty clear to me that you were calling for help.'

'Oh God! So I did . . . Oh no . . .'

Your kingdom come
Your will be done
On earth as in heaven

'Hello, it's me again, God.'

'Yes, my child, I am listening . . .'

'I was just thinking about this kingdom business. I realize it is quite scary. If I pray "your kingdom to come" that implies it has not come yet, and therefore we need to change things. Well, not just things out there, but probably I need to change me.'

'What in particular were you thinking about?'

'Well, if your kingdom is to come, and to do that your will needs to be done, that means not my will.'

'Mmmmm . . .'

'Well, I know there are loads of things I do that are not what you would want me to do . . . and yet I still do them. Like the other day at the garage, I was so cross with that silly little man who was so pompous and full of himself, and I had a really good go at him for not serving me straight away . . .'

'He did need to check his paper work before he served you. He isn't good if he is hurried . . . he gets very flustered. He isn't great with words and numbers . . .'

'Well, I am sure he did it to annoy me . . . and he did . . . and . . . well . . .'

'A little patience and a kind word costs you nothing, and it is those tiny things that go a long way to building my kingdom. I am not asking you to change the world, just change a few things in yourself. My message to all of you is very simple: just love one another. It is a great way to build my kingdom, and it will certainly help it come, here and now, where you are.'

'I can see how your way would make a difference, but it is so hard.'

Give us today our daily bread

'God, I feel so fat. I have really stuffed my face today. I really should not have eaten that bar of chocolate. As for the cooked breakfast I had this morning . . . I have pigged out all day.'

'Why do you think that is? Don't you trust me to feed you, both today and tomorrow. There is plenty to go around if everyone shares it.'

'Oh, I know there is always more than enough. It isn't that I don't trust there is enough. I am just greedy. I always seem to want more.'

'What about all those people who do not have enough food? Do you know how much they would like to feel like you do tonight? All you do is complain, and yet you are so blessed, so fortunate to want for nothing. Might it be better to say "thank you" for how you feel rather than complaining? It seems my children are never happy. Some are so hungry that they die, and my heart weeps with them as they clutch their hollow, empty stomachs longing for something to put in them. And those children who have much more than they need complain they have eaten too much. Do you remember the last chat we had about my kingdom coming on earth, now? Well, here is one of those things you can do yourself to help build my kingdom . . . How I long for my kingdom to come here on earth, so that everyone is aware of each other's needs and shares their food.'

'So you mean no more chocolates, no more cooked breakfasts. No more . . .'

'No, I do not say that. Some chocolate and cooked breakfasts are fine. But I also say be aware of yourself and others around you, and be thankful for what you have. Break bread with others, welcome them to your table – welcome them to my table. Unless bread is broken and shared, my kingdom has no chance of being built.'

Forgive us our sins
as we forgive those who sin against us

'God, you are amazing!'

'Thank you! What's brought this on?'

'Well, I was just wondering how you can agree to forgive me for all the things I have got wrong in my life. I get things wrong so often . . . and on top of that you can also forgive everyone else! Let's face it, they do some pretty awful things sometimes.'

'Well, it doesn't work quite like that. My forgiving you needs you to forgive yourself and accept my forgiveness, and then comes an even harder bit . . . if you expect me to forgive you, I expect you to forgive others.'

'Mm, yes, I see, that does put another slant on it. So you're saying you will only forgive me if I forgive others?'

'No, my child, my forgiveness is there for you at all times, anywhere, any place. But don't you think that, if you can know my love in that way, it would be good if you behave in the same way to those whom you need to forgive?'

'What, even Fred at work? You know how he is, so rude and bossy and . . .'

'Do you remember that Jesus said you should "love your enemy" and "turn the other cheek" . . .?'

'Well, yes, but . . .'

'No, there is no "but". If you really want to live my way, and build my kingdom, I do want you to forgive those who are hard to love, even Fred. To really be free from sin you need to be free from lying, hatred, revenge, anger, bitterness spitefulness . . . Think of all the time you spend complaining about Fred, and getting in a state about him. All that time you could be my kingdom-builder. Try loving Fred, he won't know what's hit him!'

'Oh, God . . .!'

'Yes, I know, I am here . . . always.'

Lead us not into temptation
but deliver us from evil

'God, it is so tempting to cheat. It would make life so much easier.'

'Are you sure about that, my child? What if you were found out?'

'Well, I won't be. It is so easy because . . .'

'It's so tempting?'

'But I pray "lead us not into temptation", and here I am being led. Why don't you do something about it – like stop it happening and then I won't be tempted?'

'Well, I rather hope you might resist yourself, knowing it is wrong, which you clearly do. I assume that is why you are talking to me about it. Rather than my controlling you like a puppet, I would much prefer you to realize I am always here to help you. Check it out against what you know to be true. Then, if it doesn't look good, you have the choice to say, "No".'

'So is this what we mean when we pray "deliver us from evil". I need to fight evil when I come across it. Come to you, have a chat, see how it looks, check it out against your Way, and then turn away and say, "No, I won't do that." Oh well, that's easy then . . . I don't think! God, I am so glad you are there. Without you I'm not sure I could do this.'

'Well, that's all right then, because I am here always and I am not going anywhere.'

For the kingdom, the power, And the glory are yours
Now and for ever. Amen

'So I guess, God, you are pretty amazing. If we would live the way you want us to, your kingdom would be everywhere and therefore your power and your glory would be shining and overwhelming all of us and everything, and we would all want to say, "thank you", because, well, you are . . . God!'

'Thank you, my child, you are pretty amazing too . . .'

Lord, Teach Me to Pray

I cannot pray 'Our', if my faith has no room for others and their needs.

I cannot pray 'Father', if I do not demonstrate this relationship to God in my daily living.

I cannot pray 'who art in heaven', if all my interests and pursuits are in earthly things.

I cannot pray 'hallowed be thy name', if I am not striving, with God's help, to be holy.

I cannot pray 'thy kingdom come', if I am unwilling to accept God's rule in my life.

I cannot pray 'thy will be done', if I am unwilling or resentful of having it in my life.

I cannot pray 'on earth as it is in heaven', unless I am truly ready to give myself to God's service, here and now.

I cannot pray 'give us this day our daily bread', without expending honest effort for it, or if I would withhold from my neighbour the bread I receive.

I cannot pray 'forgive us our trespasses as we forgive those who trespass against us', if I continue to harbour a grudge against anyone.

I cannot pray 'lead us not into temptation', if I deliberately choose to remain in a situation where I am likely to be tempted.

I cannot pray 'deliver us from evil', if I am not prepared to fight evil with my life and prayer.

I cannot pray 'thine is the kingdom', if I am unwilling to obey the King.

I cannot pray 'thine is the power and the glory', if I am seeking power for myself and my own glory first.

I cannot pray 'forever and ever', if I am anxious about each day's affairs.

I cannot pray 'Amen', unless I honestly say, 'Cost what it may, this is my prayer.'

ANON

TRADE JUSTICE

Websites	www.cafod.org.uk, www.christianaid.org.uk www.tearfund.org.uk, www.fairtrade.org.uk www.traidcraft.co.uk
Book	*Trade Justice – a Christian response to global poverty*
You will need	• CD player • CD *It Takes a Whole Village* by the African Children's Choir • A large laminated map of the world • A low table large enough to lay the map on • A basket of nightlights • Tapers • Leaflets about trade justice from one of the above organiz- ations – one for each person • Enough service sheets for everyone
Preparation	Arrange chairs in a circle if possible, add prayer stools, rugs and cushions. Place the map on the table in the centre – if necessary fix it down so it is safe. Place the basket of nightlights and the tapers nearby. Place a trade justice leaflet inside each service sheet.

Your kingdom come, your will be done.

Matthew 6.10

Welcome	Welcome. We have themed this evening's prayer and reflection on trade justice. The Trade Justice Campaign (**MakePovertyHistory**)

has grown out of Jubilee 2000, the campaign to cancel the backlog of unpayable debt owed by the poorest countries, and the Fair Trade Movement, and is a further response to the terrible imbalance of wealth in the world caused by exploitation of developing countries. The situation has become critical. Now is the time to redress the imbalance and work for fairer trade rules and agreements between rich and poor. There is a leaflet in your service sheet – please take it home and look at it.

Song

Longing for light (Christ, be our light)
(*Hymns Old and New: One church, one faith, one Lord*)
OR
Beauty for brokenness
(*The Source*)

Reading

Exodus 22.25–27

Silence

This will last about 10 minutes

Song

Inspired by love and anger
(*Iona Abbey Music Book*)
OR
Open our eyes
(*New Start Hymns and Songs*)

Reading

Luke 3.10–14

Silence

Lasting a few minutes

Song

The kingdom of God
(*Songs from Taizé*)
OR
Ubi caritas Deus ibi est
(*Songs from Taizé*)

Reading

James 5.1–6

Silence	*Lasting a few minutes*
Prayers	**Words of Wisdom** (*Jan Berry from* Harvest for the World, *Christian Aid*)

Between each prayer sing
Kindle a flame
(*Heaven Shall Not Wait*)
OR
Jesus Christ, Son of God
(*Come All You People*)

Wisdom is speaking with words of longing
for peaceful living under clear skies,
for growing crops and water fit to drink,
for just wages and fair prices in exchange for goods.
Wisdom is speaking in the voice of the poor:
Forgive us; we have failed to hear and to understand.
Sung response

Wisdom is speaking with words of challenge;
inviting us to penitence in place of self-righteousness,
calling us to move from sympathy to solidarity,
demanding justice rather than charity.
Wisdom is speaking in the voice of the poor:
forgive us; we have failed to hear and to understand.
Sung response

Wisdom is speaking with words of comfort;
offering forgiveness for our greed and affluence,
assuring us that our reckless rush to devastation
can be halted and our care of the earth restored.
Wisdom is speaking in the voice of the poor:
forgive us; we have failed to hear and to understand.
Sung response

Wisdom is speaking with words of hope;
promising us that we and the earth can be one,

inspiring us with faith in the power of people working
together,
giving us a new vision of partnership and co-operation.
Wisdom is speaking in the voice of the poor:
forgive us; we have failed to hear and to understand.
Sung response

Help us to hear and to understand
that we may share the salvation of the God of the poor.

The Lord's Prayer

Recorded Music   Let there be peace (African Children's Choir)

Action   *You are invited to come forward to place a lighted candle
                      somewhere on the map of the world – it is not too late for
                      God's redeeming light to shine in the darkness*

Song   **Jubilee Song**
                      (*Restless Is the Heart*)
                      OR
                      Send down fire
                      (*Tales of Wonder*)

*Serve fairly traded coffee and snacks – and, if possible, have a stall of Traidcraft
goods for sale. If you are not a fair trader find out who your local 'sale or return'
rep. is and make contact*

WATER

Websites   www.oxfam.org.uk, www.givewater.org,
                www.aquaid.co.uk, www.christian-aid.org.uk,
                www.cafod.org.uk

Each station will need

- Nightlights and candles in and among the items being displayed
- Several copies of the given Bible texts written on card, for people to pick up and read
- Low tables as necessary
- The items listed to illustrate each station
- Chairs, cushions, prayer stools

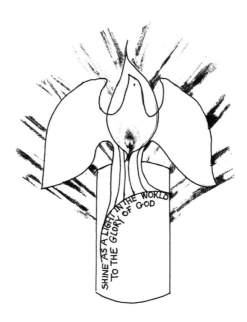

Station 1	**Baptism**
Items needed	Cards with **Mark 1.9 –11** written on them

Large bowl of water with a sign inviting people to sign themselves with the sign of the cross

Large bowl of water with a sign inviting people to wash their hands and a towel

Some words from the Common Worship Service of Baptism written on card: 'I baptize you in the name of the Father, and of the Son and of the Holy Spirit'

or

'This is our faith. We believe and trust in one God, Father, Son and Holy Spirit'

Cards for people to take away saying: 'Shine as a light in the world to the glory of God the Father'. See the Shine as a light template at the back of the book, page 184

Station 2	**Drinking Water**
Items needed	Cards with **John 4.13–14** written on them

Large jug of water with drinking cups

Sign inviting people to take a drink

Information about how many people in the world do not have clean drinking water:

> 43 countries face severe water shortages
>
> 1.2 billion people lack access to safe water, which leads to the death of 2.2 million people each year
>
> 600 million small-scale rural farmers lack sufficient water for their subsistence and livelihoods

2 litre bottles of water, this is what many people have to live on every day for their drinking, bathing and washing (why not challenge yourself to live for one day with only 2 litres of water in solidarity with those who have no choice?)

Card with a list of water-related diseases: Cholera, Dysentery, Typhoid Fever, Bilharzia, and Worms

Card to take away with 'Thank you, God, for clean water' written on it. See the Thank you God template at the back of the book, page 185

Station 3	**Weather and Crops**
Items needed	Cards with **Psalm 29 or 65.9–13** written on them
	A selection of clothes related to the weather – mackintosh, hat, gloves, wellington boots and umbrella
	Prayer cards with words of thanksgiving for wonderful weather
	Prayer cards with words of concern for those affected negatively by the weather, maybe as a result of events going on in the world at the moment, eg floods, droughts, tornadoes, hurricanes. See the Floods etc template and the Hail etc template at the back of the book, pages 186 and 187
	Things to illustrate the staple crops of the world eg rice, wheat, maize . . .
	Some fruit and vegetables

Station 4	**The Sea**
Items needed	Cards with **Luke 8.22–25** written on them
	Cards with **Luke 5.1–11** written on them
	Cards with **John 21.1–14** written on them
	Large plastic sheet laid out on the floor on which to build the 'seaside'. Thin blue fabric laid on the plastic to look like rippling water

Sand to be the beach

Shells, rocks, seaweed

A rockpool made with a bowl disguised by rocks

Buckets and spades

Fishing nets, fish and an unlit barbecue with pitta bread and cooked fish

A card inviting people to eat

Deckchairs to sit on, towels to lie on, sun oil, sunglasses

CD player

CD of sea sounds

Station 5

Items needed

Tears

Psalm 126.5–6 or **John 11.35** written on them

Pictures of people grieving – either cut out from the press or printed off the Internet or as a PowerPoint presentation

Prayer cards in the shapes of tears for naming people or situations to be prayed for

String suspended between two points to hang the 'tear' prayer cards on. See the tear template at the back of the book, page 188

'. . . but those who drink of the water that
I will give them will never be thirsty'

John 4.14

Welcome

We are here this evening to stop and reflect on water. Something we so often take for granted in our lives. We turn on a tap without thinking twice about it. We use the washing machine, dishwasher, garden hose or run a long, hot, deep bath, without praising God for the wonder and gift of water. When did you last stop and really reflect on the wateriness of water? To see the sun bounce off the surface of the sea sparkling like diamonds. To notice the dew caught in a spider's web, or stand in the pouring rain and really be soaked to the skin.

To help us really reflect on the wonder of water, there are five places to stop, think, wonder and pray placed around the building. They are in no particular order. Use them in your own time and way. You might drink the water, splash or wash your hands in it or just feel it running through your fingers.

Of course, too much or too little water can have a terrible effect on people's lives. So take the time to pray for those who long for enough water, or who long for the floods to end.

The Bible stories chosen reflect on some of the moments when Jesus mentioned or used water, or when water is mentioned, particularly in the psalms. Jesus used water as an illustration for the cleansing of our sins, the ever-present hope offered to us of starting again.

The quiet reflective time will be about 45 minutes. At the end of that time we will all stop and come together for the last few moments when we will pray and sing before we leave.

At the end   At the end of each intercession there is a short response followed by 'Amen'. This is a word we say so often in our prayers. But how often do we really think about what it means? When we say 'Amen' we are affirming what has been said: 'Let it be so', or 'Here, here', 'I agree', 'Certainly'. So let us say it as if we mean it.

Let us pray to the Lord:

For the wonder and wetness of water
For puddles to splash in, and the joy of mud pies
Praise God. Amen

For weather: rain, snow, sleet, hail and the power of thunder and lightning
Praise God. Amen

For baptism, and the chance to say 'sorry' and to start again. For being washed whiter than snow, in fact to be washed so clean that we can be challenged to 'shine as a light in God's world',
Praise God. Amen

For the blessing of not having to think about where our next drink of water will come from
For the blessing of running water in our houses

For bottled water in our shops
For washing machines and garden hoses
Praise God. Amen

For the sea, so powerful and yet also so gentle
For the wonder of God's creation, fish of many colours, whales, dolphins
For seaside holidays to refresh and rejuvenate
Praise God. Amen

For those who risk their lives at sea for our sake
We thank you, God. Amen

For those who have nowhere dry to go, no shelter or protection from the weather
May they find hope. Amen

For those who long for some clean water, and those who try to change the world so they can have some
We pray we will respond and do all we can to help, being generous with our time and money. Amen

For all who grow crops to feed themselves and others
We ask for God's blessing upon them. Amen

For those who will cry alone tonight, with no one to be with them
Let them find comfort. Amen

For those who shed tears because someone has died
Let them find comfort. Amen

We all praise God for the wonder of life-giving water, and for Jesus, the well-spring of Life.
Amen and Amen! Praise God!

Song
The Lord is my song
(*Songs and Prayers from Taizé*)
OR
My soul is thirsting
(*Go Before Us*)

WORLD PEACE

You will need
- CD player
- CD of *The Armed Man: A mass for peace* by Karl Jenkins
- A large cross laid down on the floor with the head lifted up higher than the foot
- Candles of varying sizes
- Nightlights in a basket, matches or tapers
- Words on cards with the names of countries/places/situations which need praying for – some of these placed on low tables
- A large sign saying, 'Nation will not take up sword against nation, nor will they train for war any more.'
- Service sheets for everyone

Preparation
Make a focal point with the large cross and lighted candles.
Place the seating around the cross in a semi-circle.
Place the nightlights and tapers in a basket near the foot of the cross.

**Nation will not take up sword against nation,
nor will they train for war any more.**

Micah 4.3

Welcome
The theme for this evening is peace. Peace in this troubled world; peace in all places where wars are happening and in places where wars have happened and bitterness and hatred still prevail; peace in our own communities and peace in our homes and families. Running through the service will be some of the music from *The Armed Man: A mass for peace* by Karl Jenkins. The service will not be a mass, but rather a time, using

some of the music, Bible readings and silence to reflect on war and the damage it does, and to pray for peace – to take time to see how each of us in our own small way can make peace happen both in our own hearts and the communities we live in. The words being sung are written down in the service sheet so they can be followed along with the music.

Silence

Music

The Armed Man
(*Composer Karl Jenkins based on* L'Homme Armé *written 1450–63 anon. trad. Sung in French*)
The armed man must be feared;
Everywhere it has been decreed
That every man should arm himself
With an iron coat of mail.

Silence

Reflection

Paul says in his Letter to the Ephesians 6.14 and 15:
'So stand ready, with truth as a belt tight round your waist, with righteousness as your breastplate, and as your shoes the readiness to announce the Good News of peace.'
But we wrap ourselves up in 'iron coats of mail', and we arm ourselves with weapons to kill. We do not choose to live the Good News way of peace, but rather the bad news way of wars, killing, hatred, death and destruction. Every generation fails to see how hatred only leads to more hatred, more killing, more sorrow. We arm ourselves to fight each other, to kill each other, to pass on the hatred from one generation to the next. Fight, kill, hate, kidnap, murder, and destroy . . .
The guidance we are given in the Bible is not to dress ourselves in 'iron coats of mail', but rather we are told in Ephesians 6.11 and 14–18 to

> put on the full armour of God . . . Stand firm then, with the belt of truth buckled round your waist, with the breastplate of righteousness in place, and with your feet fitted with the readiness that comes from the gospel of peace. In addition to

all this, take up the shield of faith, with which you can extinguish all the flaming arrows of the evil one. Take the helmet of salvation and the sword of the Spirit, which is the word of God.

Silence

Prayer   Lord, have mercy and forgive us,
Response   **Lord, have mercy and forgive us.**
                   Christ, have mercy and forgive us,
                   Christ, have mercy and forgive us.
                   Lord, have mercy and forgive us,
                   Lord, have mercy and forgive us.

Silence

Music   **Charge!**
                   Composer: Karl Jenkins; words: Song for St Cecilia's Day *(1687) by John Dryden (1631–1700). To the Earl of Oxford after Horace by Jonathan Swift (1667–1745)*
                   Published by Boosey and Hawkes Music Publishers Ltd

                   The trumpet's loud clangour
                   Excites us to Arms
                   With shrill notes of Anger
                   And mortal Alarms
                   Dryden
                   How blest is he who for his country dies
                   Swift
                   The double double beat
                   Of the thundering drum
                   Cries, Hark the Foes come;
                   Charge, Charge, 'tis too late to retreat
                   Dryden
                   How blest is he who for his country dies
                   Swift
                   Charge, charge
                   Dryden

Silence

Music	**Agnus Dei**
	Composer: Karl Jenkins; words: Ordinary of the Mass

Published by Boosey and Hawkes Music Publishers Ltd.

Sung in Latin
O Lamb of God, that takes away the sins of the world,
grant us Thy peace.

Silence	

Reading	**Micah 4.2–4**

Many nations will come and say,
'Come, let us go up to the mountain of the Lord,
to the house of the God of Jacob.
He will teach us his ways,
so that we may walk in his paths.'
The law will go out from Zion,
the word of the Lord from Jerusalem.
He will judge between many peoples
and will settle disputes for strong nations far and wide.
They will beat their swords into ploughshares
and their spears into pruning hooks.
Nation will not take up sword against nation,
Nor will they train for war any more.
Every man will sit under his own vine
and under his own fig-tree,
and no one will make them afraid,
for the Lord Almighty has spoken.

Song	**Sing, praise and bless the Lord (Laudate Dominum)**
	(Songs fromTaizé)
	OR
	My peace
	(Be Still and Know)

*While the song is being sung quietly, everyone is invited to
come forward and light a candle to place by each of the cards*

arranged around the cross. Gradually the candles will bring light to the area, symbolically bringing God's light into the dark situations of the world

Music

Better is Peace
Composer: Karl Jenkins; words: Le Morte d'Arthur *(1469–70) by Sir Thomas Malory (?–1471); from* In Memoriam A.A.H. *(1850) by Alfred Lord Tennyson (1809–92)*
The Book of Revelation from the Bible

Lancelot: Better is peace than always war
Guinevere: And better is peace than evermore war.
Malory
The Armed Man must be feared;
Everywhere it has been decreed
That every man should arm himself
With an Iron Coat of mail
Ring out the thousand wars of old,
Ring in the thousand years of peace.
Ring out the old, ring in the new,
Ring, happy bells, across the snow:
The year is going, let him go;
Ring out the false, ring in the true.
Ring out old shapes and foul disease;
Ring out the narrowing lust of gold;
Ring out the thousand wars of old,
Ring in the thousand years of peace.
Ring in the valiant man and free,
The larger heart, the kindlier hand;
Ring out the darkness of the land;
Ring in the Christ that is to be.
Tennyson
. . . God shall wipe away all tears . . .
And there shall be no more death
Neither sorrow nor crying
Neither shall there be any more pain
Revelations 21.4
Praise the Lord

Blessing

O God of Peace, let our hearts long for your peace,
O God of Light, let your light lighten the dark places of the world,
Oh God of Hope, let those who feel hopeless find your encouragement,
Oh God of Comfort, let those full of sorrow and grief feel your loving embrace,
Oh God of Love, do not despair of your children, but fill our world and your world with your love, comfort, hope, light and peace.
Amen

ILLUSTRATIONS

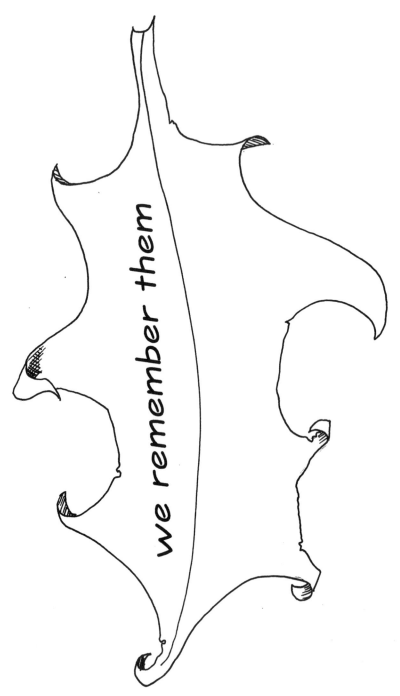

we remember them

For use with the All Souls service, page 41

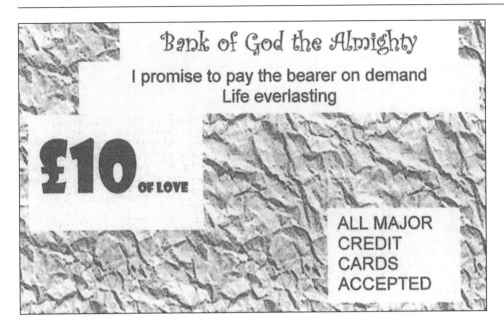

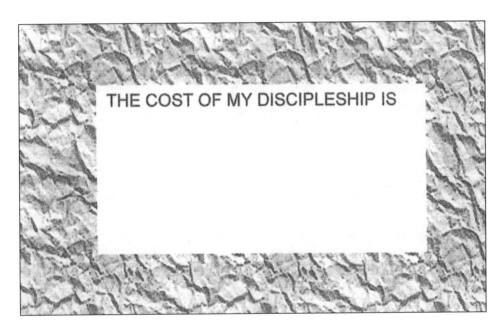

For use with the Cost of Discipleship service, page 65

Write
here

Instructions for Epiphany gift wrapping
1 Cut a small (roughly 7 x 9 cm) rectangular piece of wrapping paper – make
   sure the reverse side is white and can be written on.
2 Fold it three times, lengthways and crossways.
3 Fold it into a square and tuck the ends in.
4 Draw a ribbon on the front.
5 Each person will need one.

For use with the Epiphany service, page 73

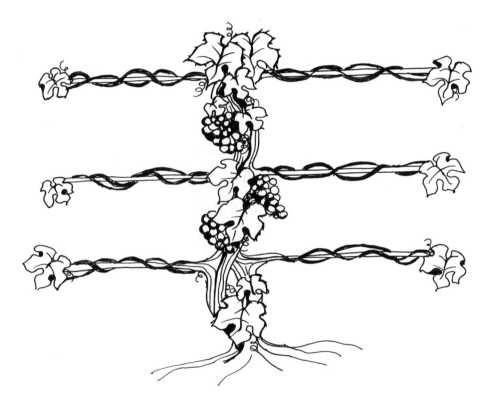

For use with the Families service, page 76

For use with the Families service, page 76

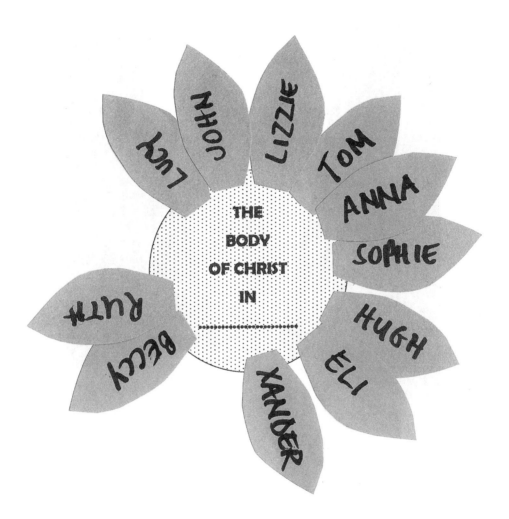

Illustration to show how to make a sunflower for the Harvest of the Body of Christ service, page 79

For use with the Holy Week service, page 92

Illustration to show how to make cards and chains for use with the Peace service, page 117

For use with the Peace service, page 117

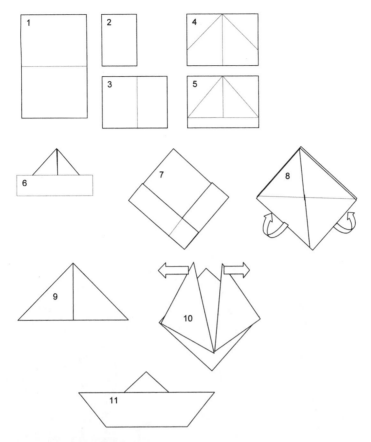

HOW TO MAKE A PAPER BOAT

 1 Take a sheet of A4 paper and fold it in half from top to bottom.
2/3 Fold it in half the other way and make a good crease, then open it up
    again.
 4 Fold the corners to the middle creased line with opening at bottom.
5/6 Fold the spare paper at the bottom up on each side.
 7 Tuck the little flaps inside, take hold of the centre crease on each side,
    pull open and crease edges.
 8 With the open edge at the bottom fold the bottom point to the top.
    Turn over and repeat on the other side.
 9 Holding the middle creases open out and flatten the opposite way.
10 Take hold of the two top points and pull the boat open.
11 Have fun *floating* the boat!

For use with the Pentecost service, page 122

For use with the Prisoners service, page 125

For use with the Remembrance service, page 135

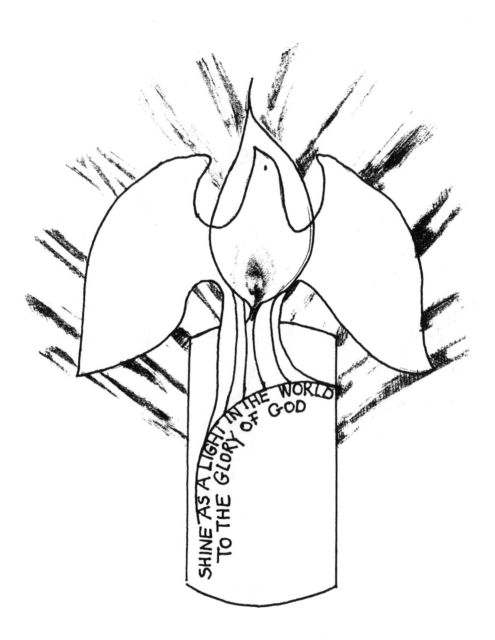

SHINE AS A LIGHT IN THE WORLD TO THE GLORY OF GOD

For use with the Water service, page 159

For use with the Water service, page 159

For use with the Water service, page 159

For use with the Water service, page 159

For use with the Water service, page 159